DIRT SIMPLE®

COUNTRY GUITAR

BY
JOHN HARTIN
AND CHET HARTIN

Online Audio www.melbay.com/30705MEB

MEL BAY®

WWW.MELBAY.COM

Introduction

The guitar and country music go back a long way. From the early days of the Carter Family, Jimmy Rogers, Ernest Tubb and Hank Williams to the present day, most country music has been written and sung with just a few guitar chords.

The purpose of this book is for the student to learn those basic guitar chords and accompaniment styles and begin to play the melodies with the most common picking techniques. Playing backup guitar is fun and not difficult to learn. I hope you enjoy this introduction to country music.

We have chosen these songs as they are timeless country tunes and are often played at local jams and small get-togethers.

Acknowledgements

Special thanks go out to our family. We would also like to thank Dann Tincher, Jacinda Beth, and Stuart Moody for all the additional help in completing this project.

Many thanks,

John & Chet Hartin

Table of Contents

	Page	Audio
Chords	4	
Reading Tablature	5	
Bury Me Beneath the Willow	6	1
The Columbus Stockade Blues	8	2
Just a Closer Walk with Thee	10	3
Red River Valley	12	4
The Nine-Pound Hammer	14	5
Bile Them Cabbage Down	16	6
The Worried Man Blues	18	7
Careless Love	20	8
The Crawdad Song	22	9
The Unclouded Day	24	10
Amazing Grace	26	11
In the Pines	28	12
Oklahoma Moonlight Waltz	30	13
Hand Me Down My Walking Cane	32	14
Scoot-a-Boot Boogie	34	15
Lone Star Country	36	16
Foggy Mountain Top	38	17
Old-Time Religion	40	18
Under the Double Eagle	41	19
Wildwood Flower	42	20

Chords

Here are several chords we'll use in this book. Be sure to practice them on their own!

Major Chords

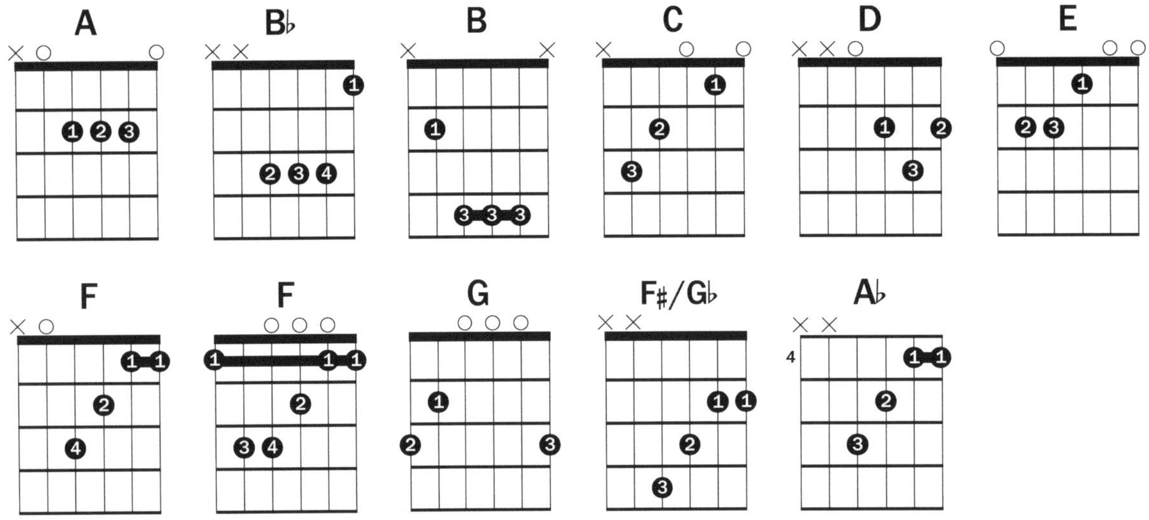

Dominant Seven Chords

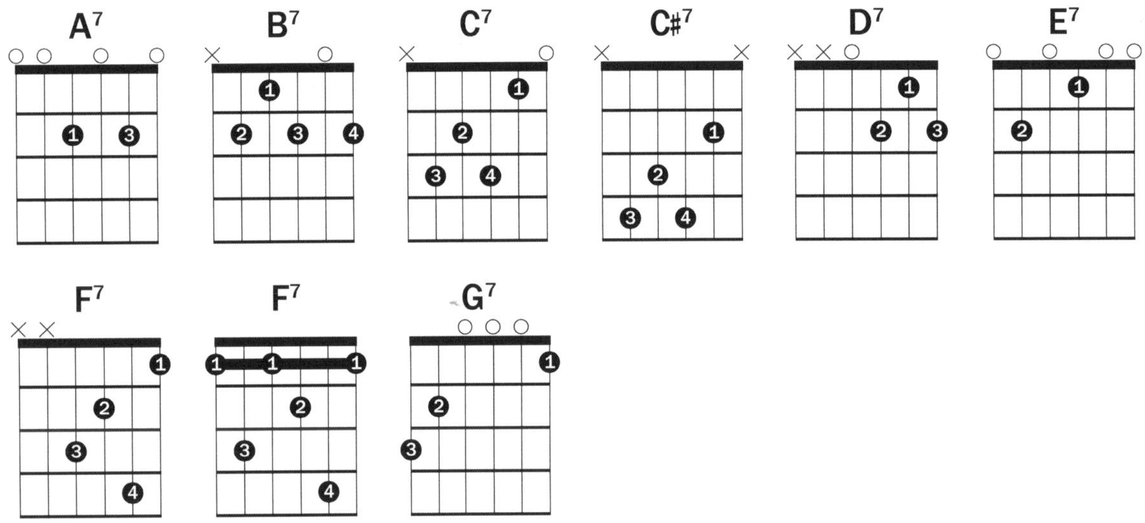

Minor Chords

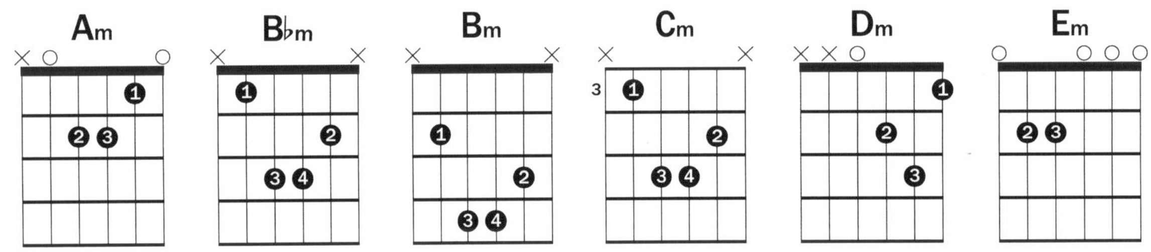

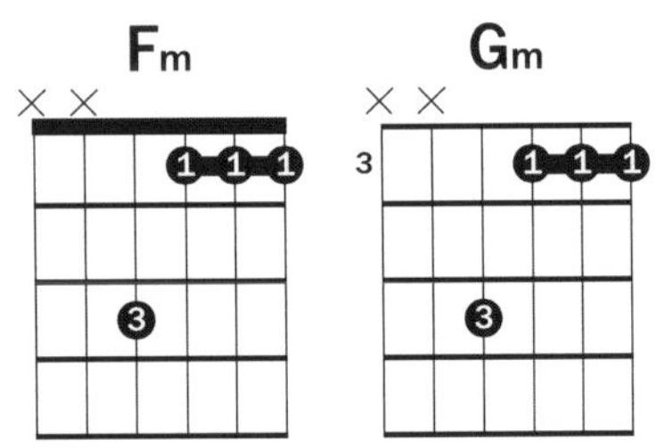

Fully Diminished 7th Chords

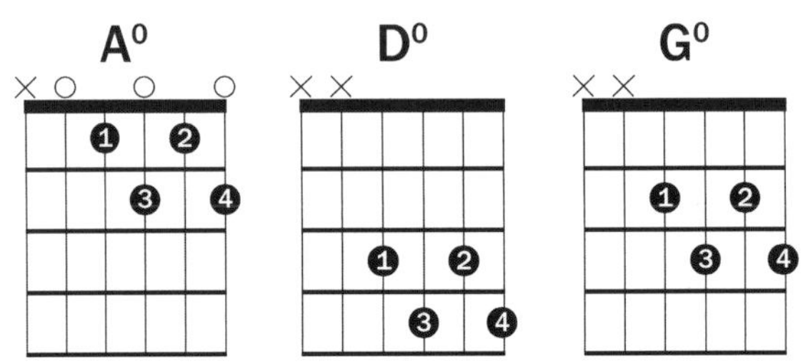

Reading Tab

You'll notice that this book uses a traditional treble clef for standard notation as well as a tablature (tab) staff. If you're new to the guitar, all of these numbers can be a little confusing.

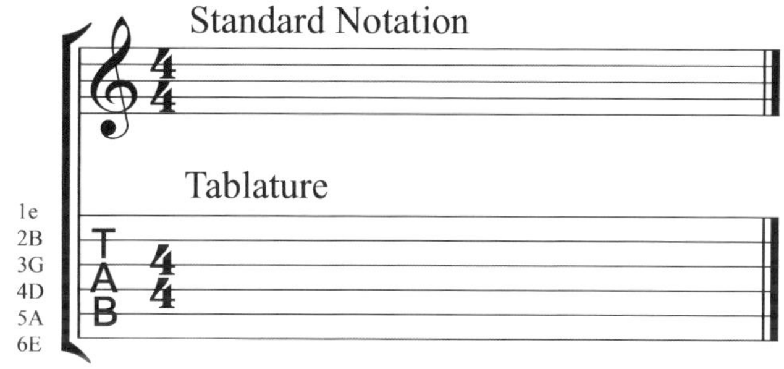

Each line of tab indicates which string to play, with 1e representing the smallest, high-pitched string on the guitar, the high E, whereas 6E represents the largest string on the guitar, the low E.

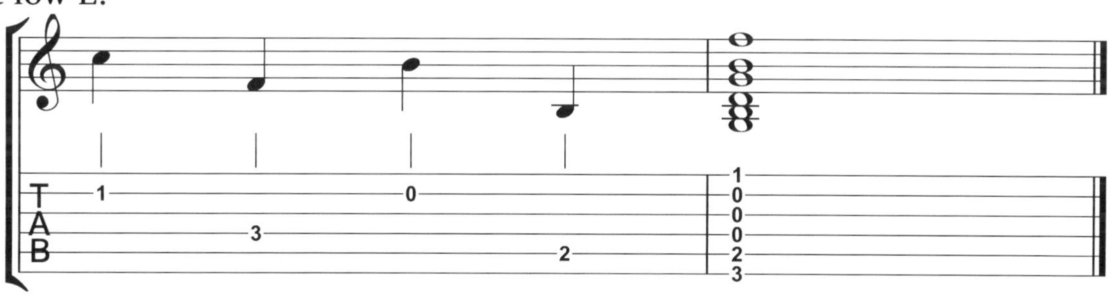

In the above sample, the numbers represent the fret where you place your fingers. The first number 1 indicates that your finger should be on the first fret on the B string. Single numbers represent a melody line or solo. The second bar is an example of a chord as indicated by the stacked numbers. A zero (O), means that there are no fingers on that string, but you should still play the open string.

Below you will find diagrams showing the meaning of numbers when applied to the left-hand fingers, and strings:

Frets

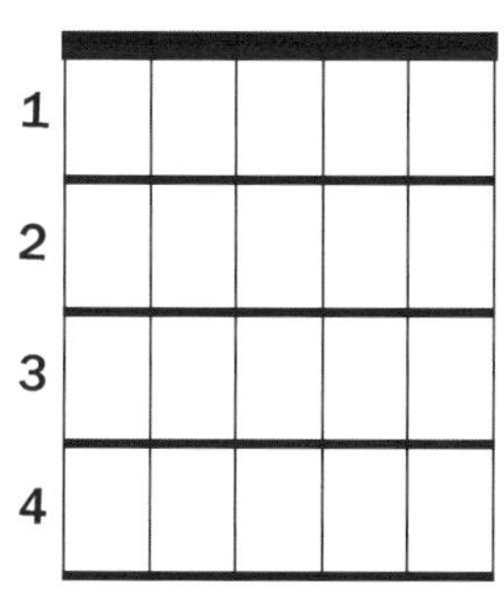

Fingers

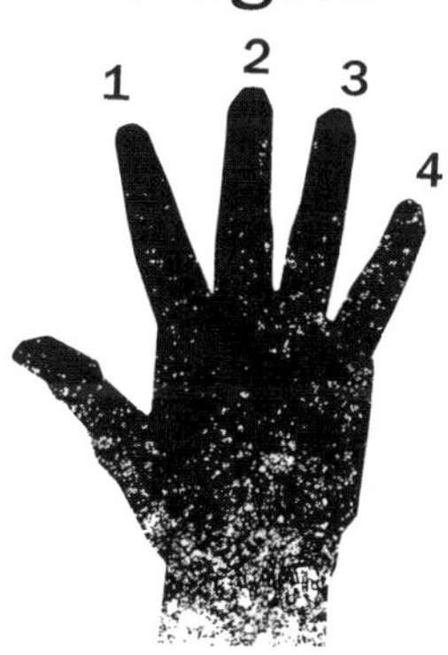

Strings

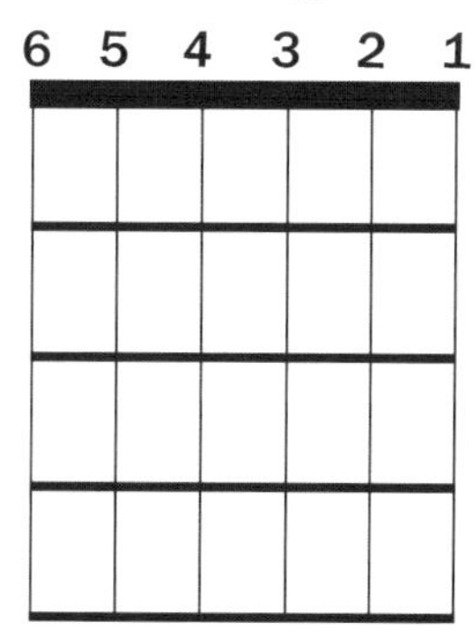

Bury Me Beneath the Willow

"Bury Me Beneath the Willow" has been performed by many country artists, including Dolly Parton, The Carter Family, Allison Krauss, and many others.

You may be wondering what the p stands for in the notation. This is short for "pull-off". When you play a note, quickly pull-off to the next lower note.

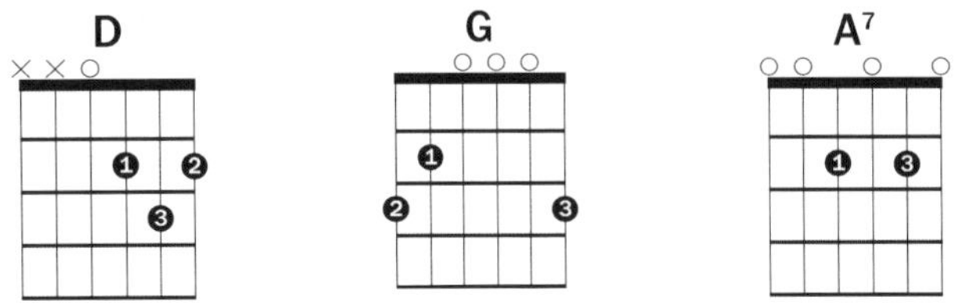

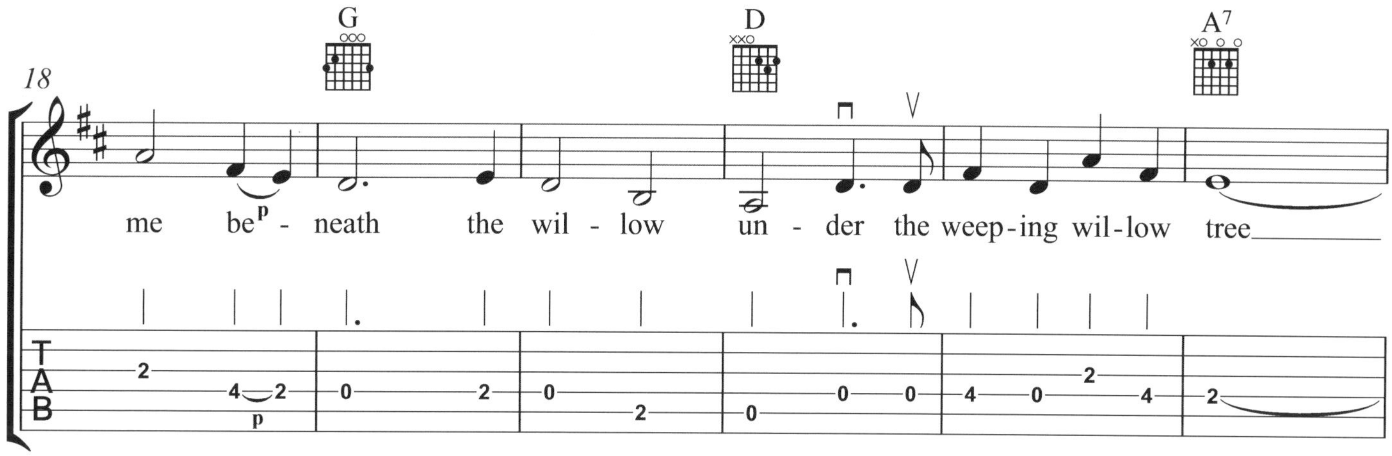

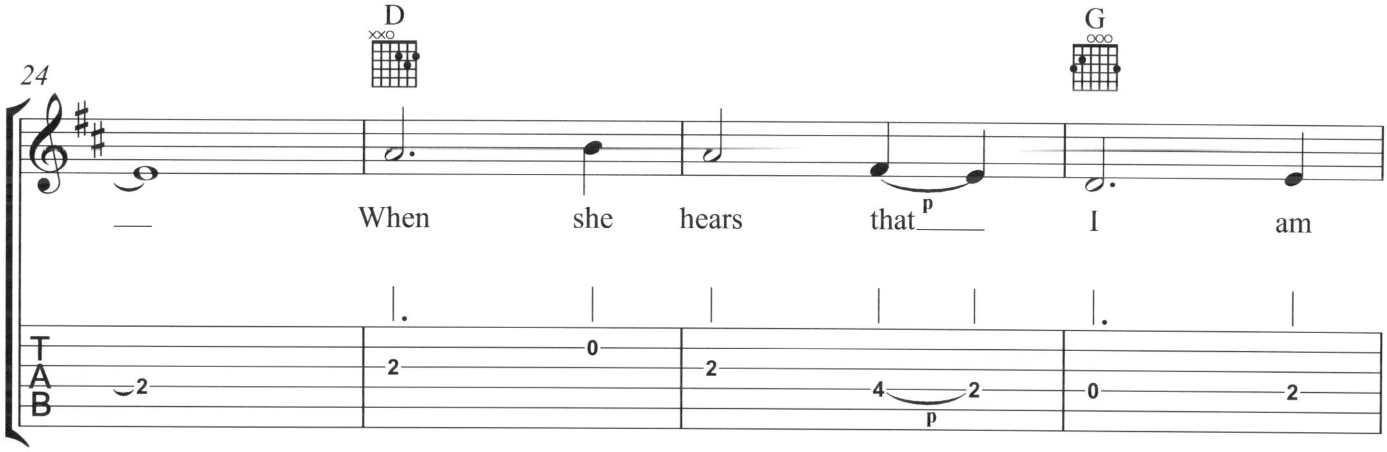

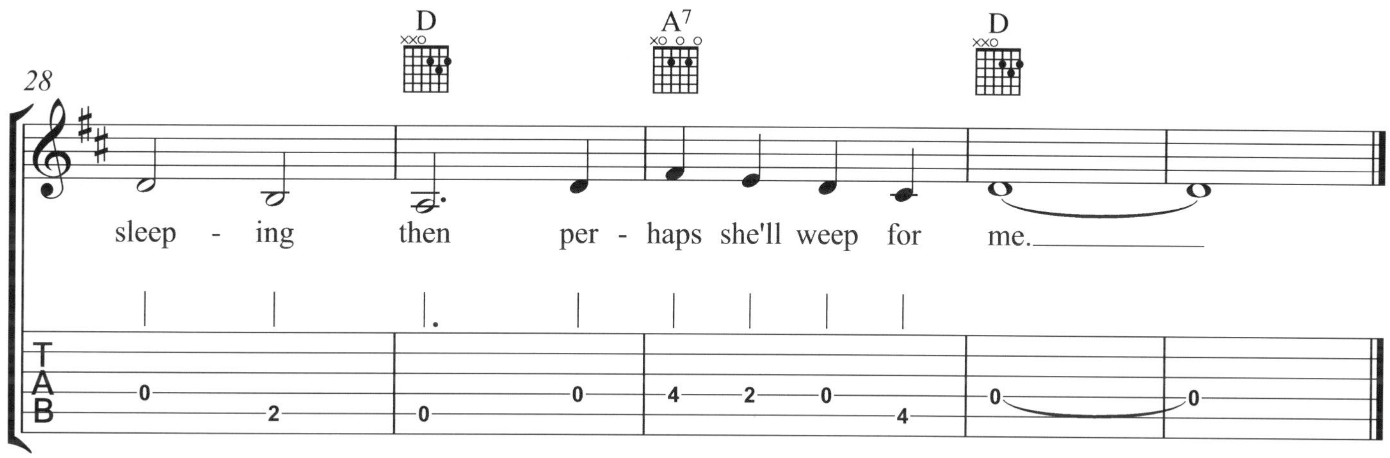

These alternate bass notes really add a lot to the accompaniment:

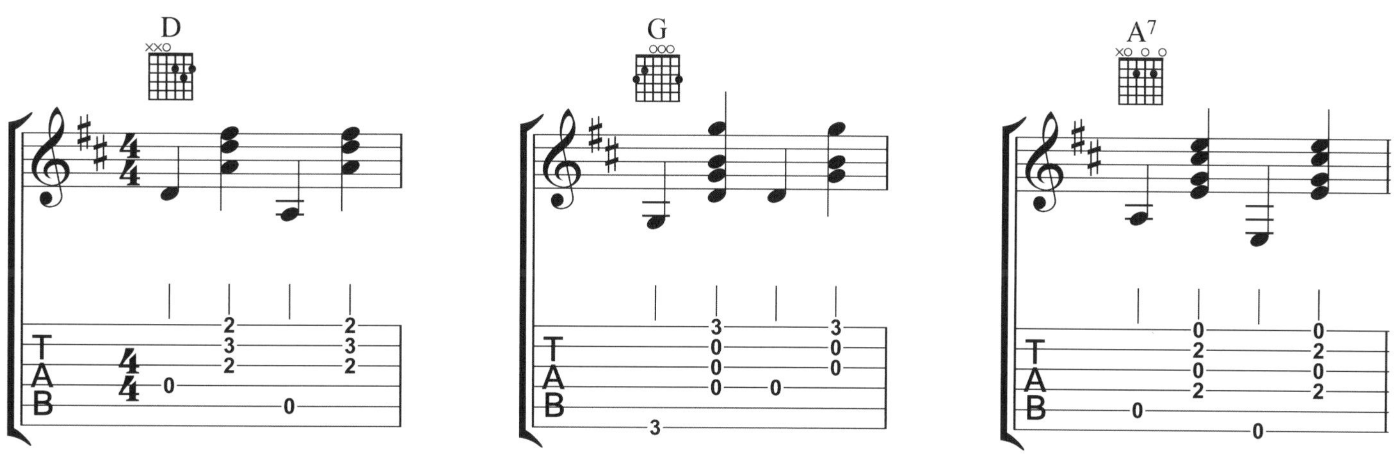

The Columbus Stockade Blues

Darby and Tarlton were an early country duo who recorded over 60 songs, many considered classics. This tune and "Birmingham Jail" sold more than 200,000 copies.

The symbol for downpicking (⊓), indicates that you play this note in a downward motion. By contrast, ∨ is the symbol for up-picking. In a series of notes, it is common to alternate picking directions.

2

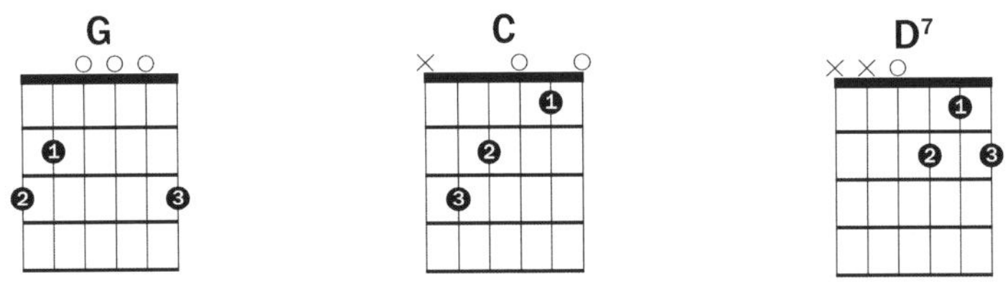

Thomas Darby
Jimmie Tarlton

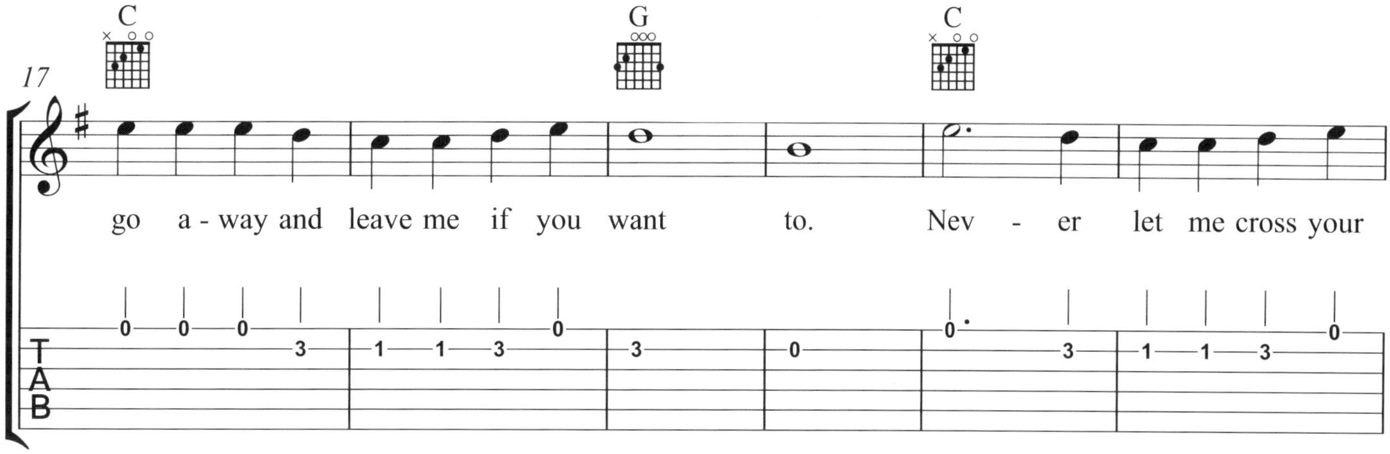

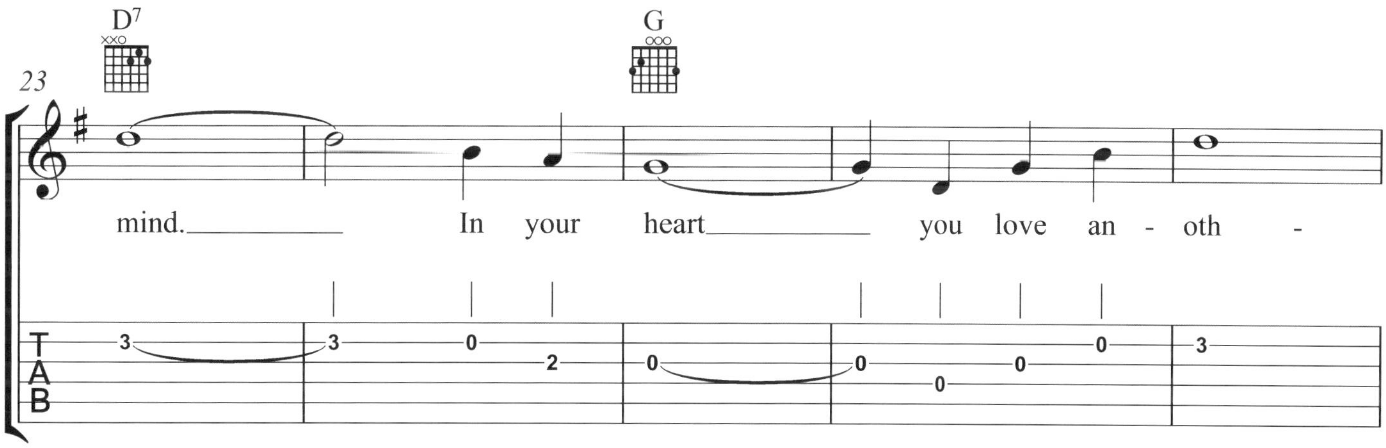

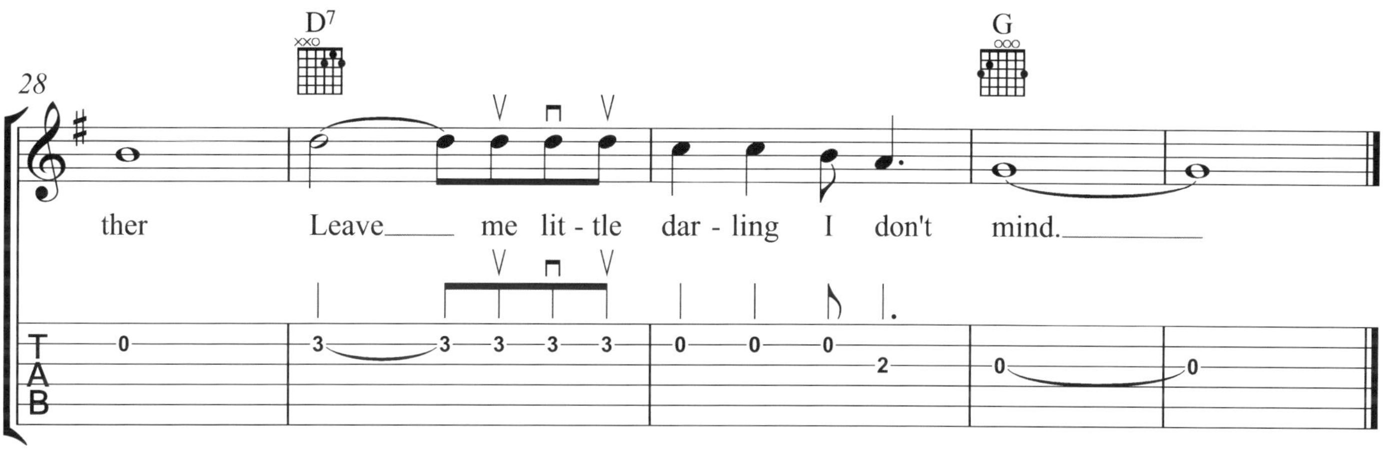

If you're playing with a friend, or don't feel like playing lead, try using these alternating bass patterns for accompaniment:

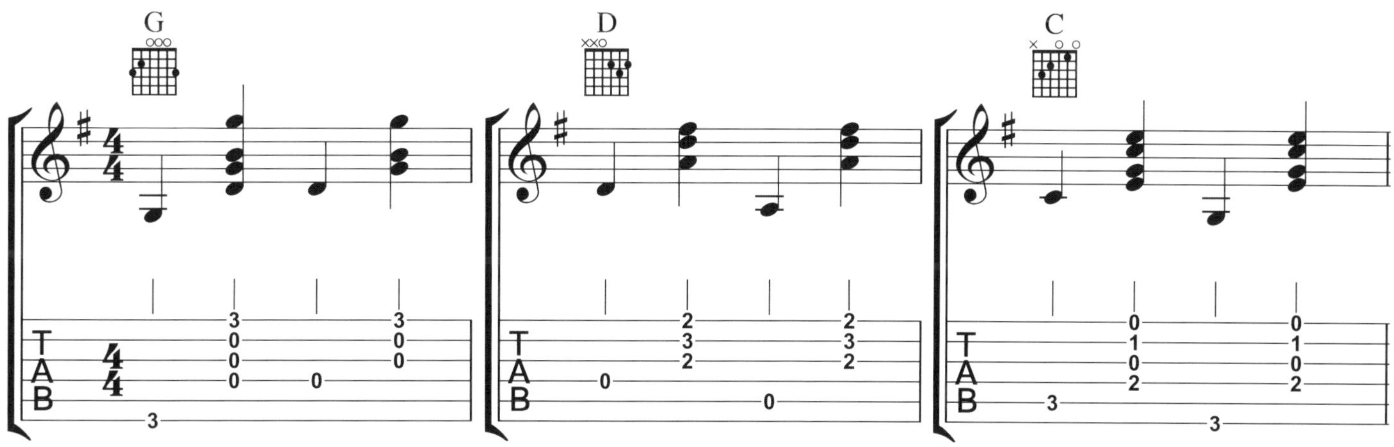

Just a Closer Walk with Thee

This song has been recorded by Patsy Cline, Anne Murray, Louis Armstrong, and Mahalia Jackson along with many other popular artists

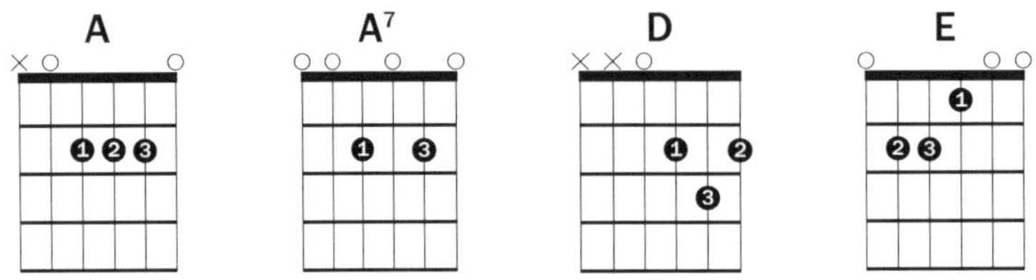

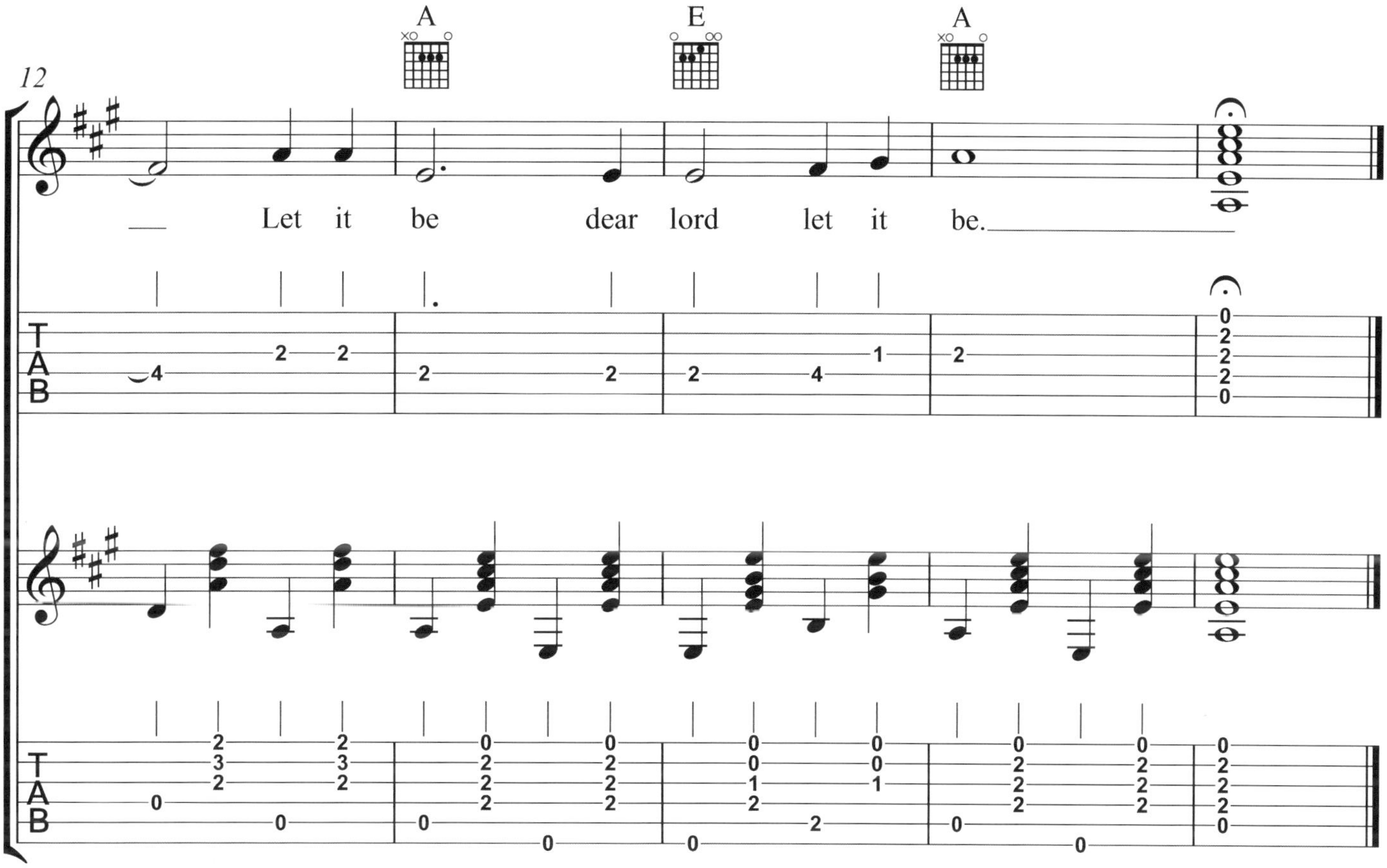

I am weak but Thou art strong
Jesus keep me from all wrong
I'll be satisfied as long
As I walk, let me walk close to Thee.

When my feeble life is o'er
Time for me will be no more
Guide me gently, safely o'er
To Thy kingdom's shore, to Thy shore.

Red River Valley

Suzy Boggus, Marty Robbins and many others have performed this beautiful western song. The melody was also used in “Can I Sleep in Your Arms, Mister” by Jeannie Seely

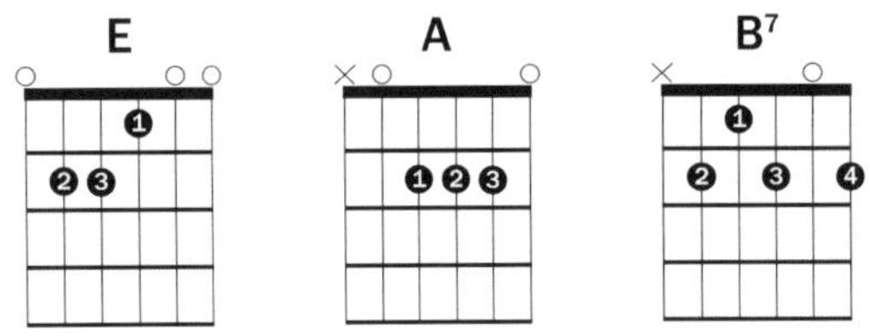

Do you think of the valley you're leavin'
Oh how lonely and dreary it will be
Do you think of the fond heart you're breakin'
And the sadness you've cast over me.

For a long time my dear, I've been waiting
For the words that you never would say
And alas my poor heart you are breakin'
For they tell me you're goin' away.

As you go to your home by the ocean
May you never forget those sweet hours
That we spent in the Red River Valley
And the love we exchanged mid the flowers.

Come and sit by my side if you love me
Do not hasten to bid me adieu
But remember the Red River Valley
And the one that has loved you so true.

The Nine-Pound Hammer

The great singer, composer and guitarist Merle Travis recorded many hit songs including this one. It has also been perfomed by Bill Monroe and the great Chet Atkins

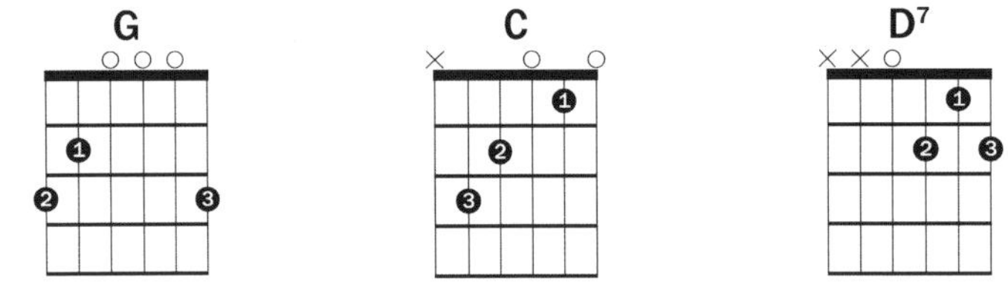

Merle Travis
arr. John Hartin

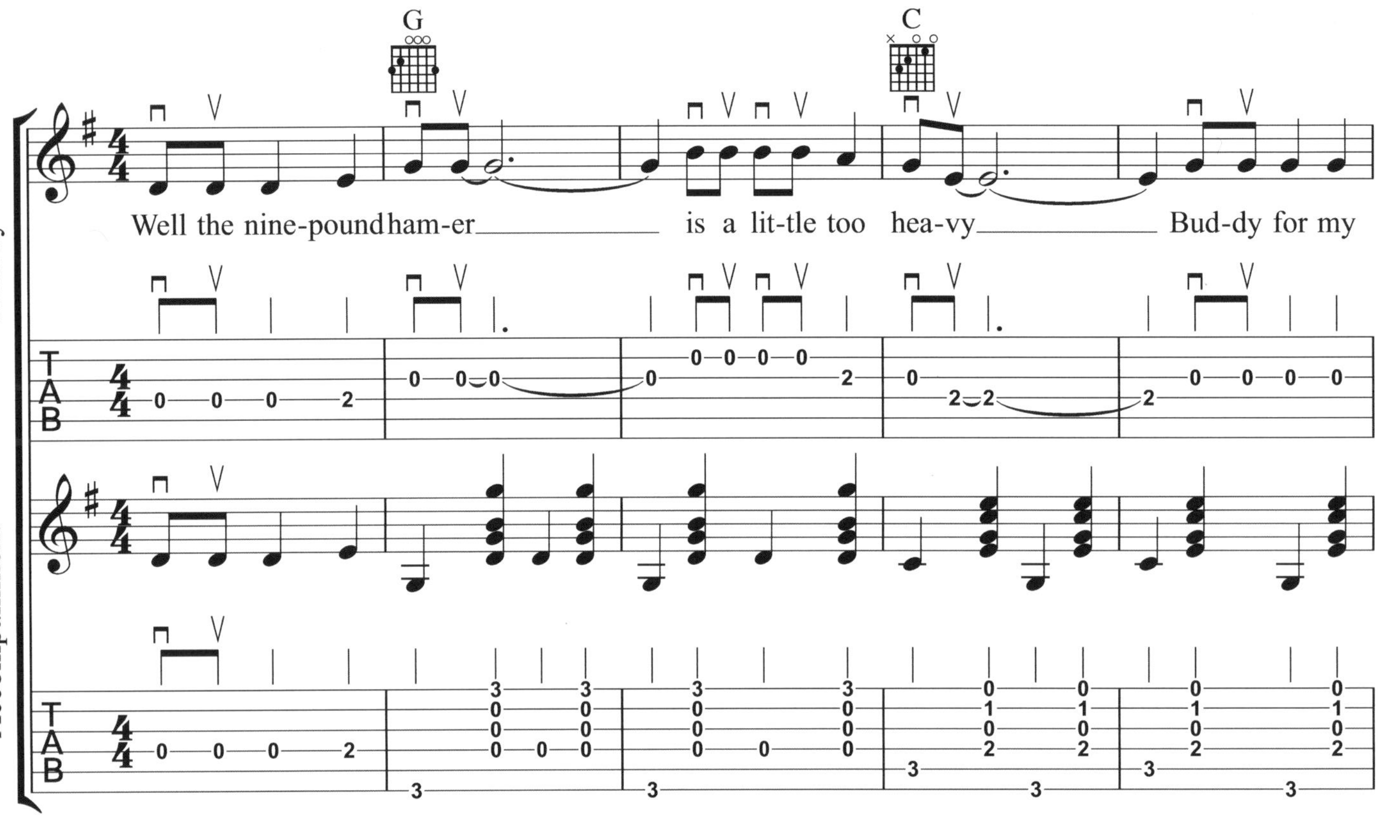

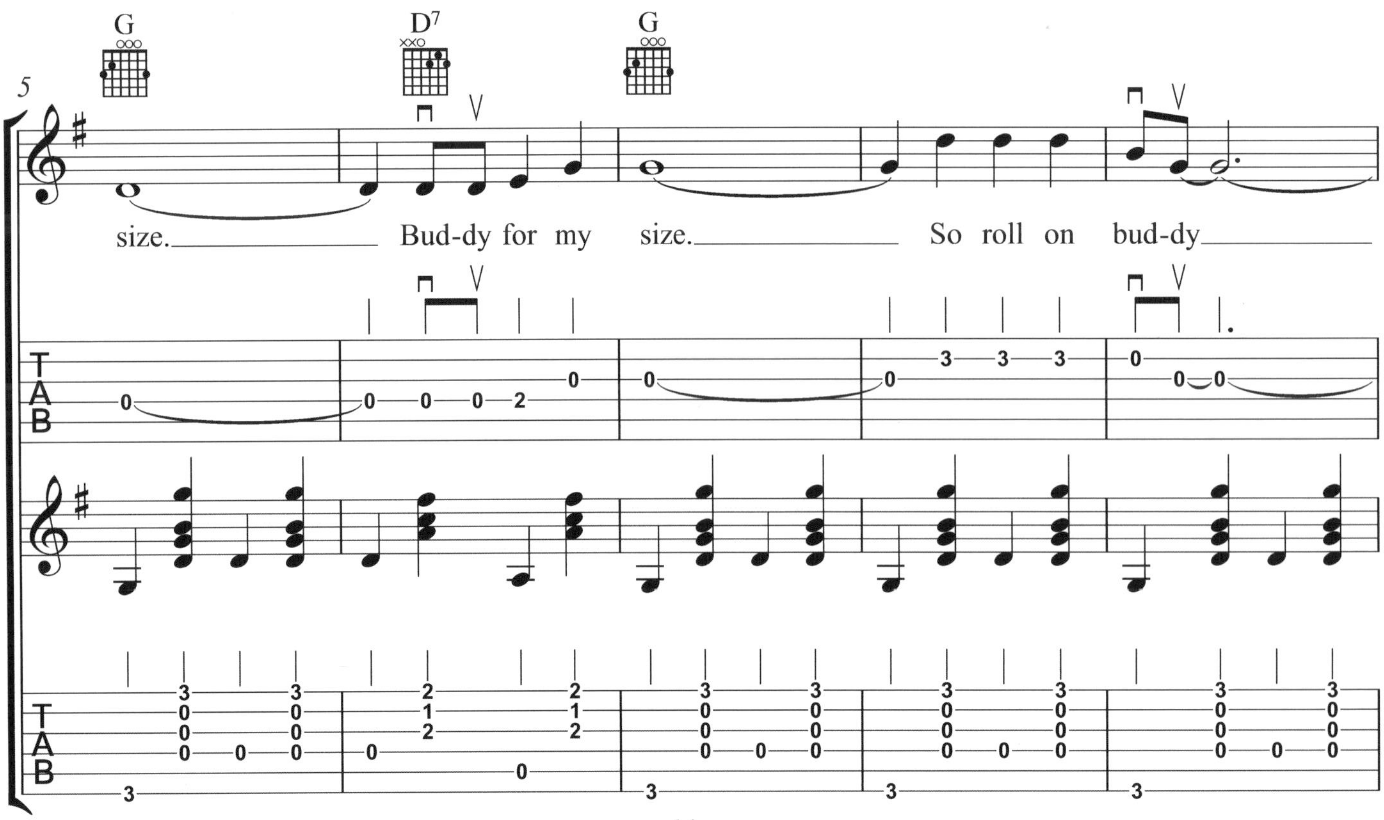

10
C
G
Don't you roll so slow
How can I roll
14
D7
G
when the whe - els won't go.

Bile Them Cabbage Down

This tune is often played on the fiddle, but it's mighty fun to play on the guitar! Notice the walking bass-runs in the accompaniment.

6

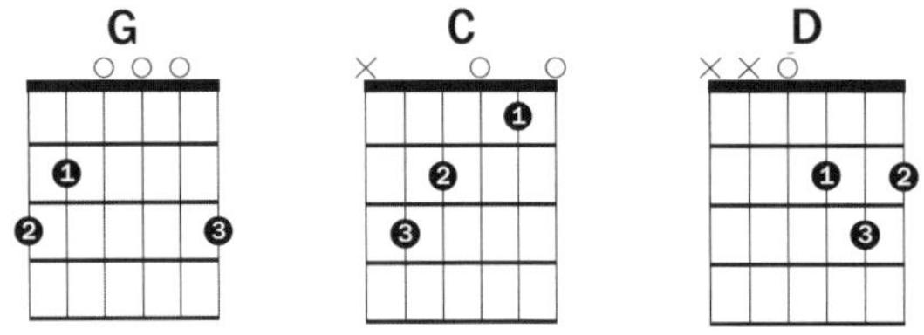

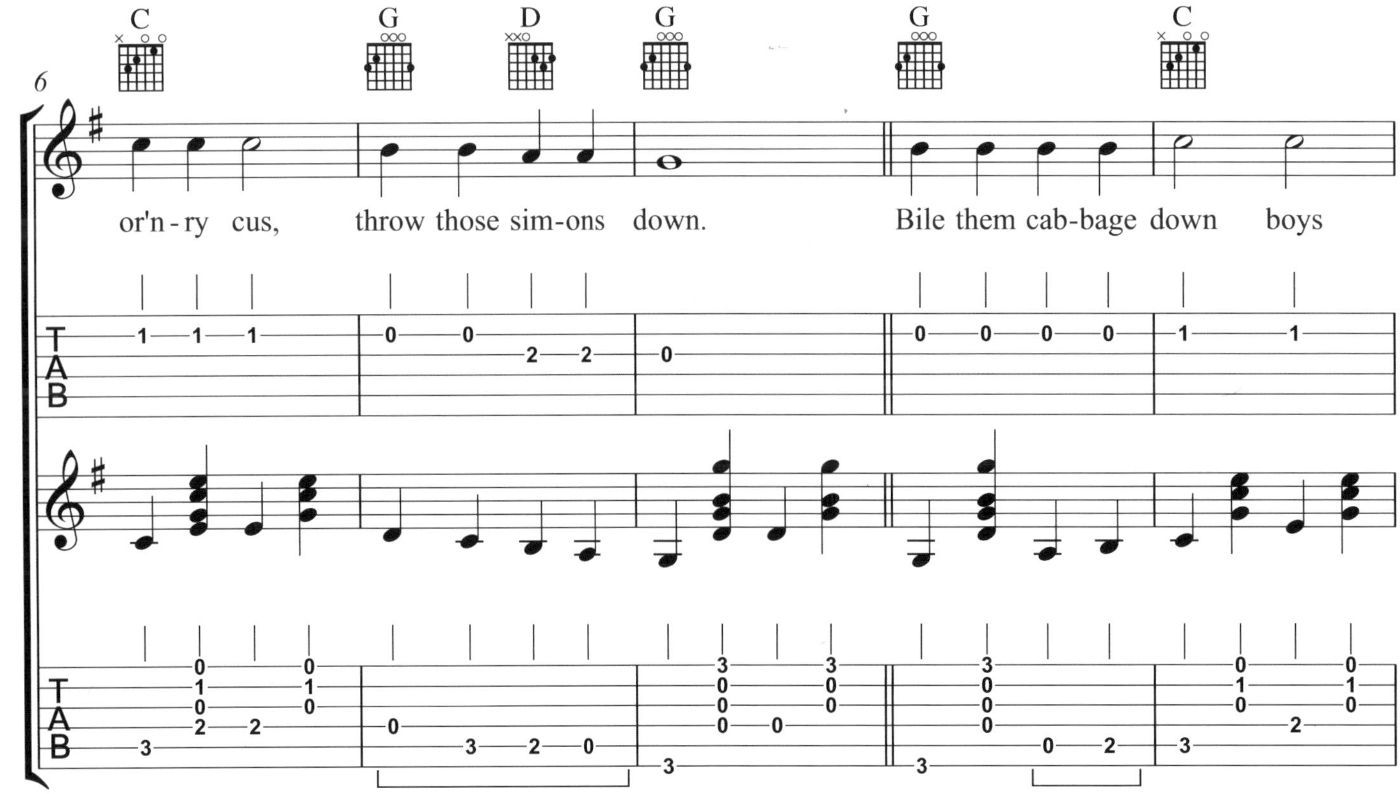

11
G
D
G
bake the hoe cake brown. The on - ly song that
14
C
G
D
G
I can sing is Bile Them Cab - bage Down.

The Worried Man Blues

The Kingston Trio had a big hit with this tune. The accompaniment is a lot of fun to play with the walking bass line.

7

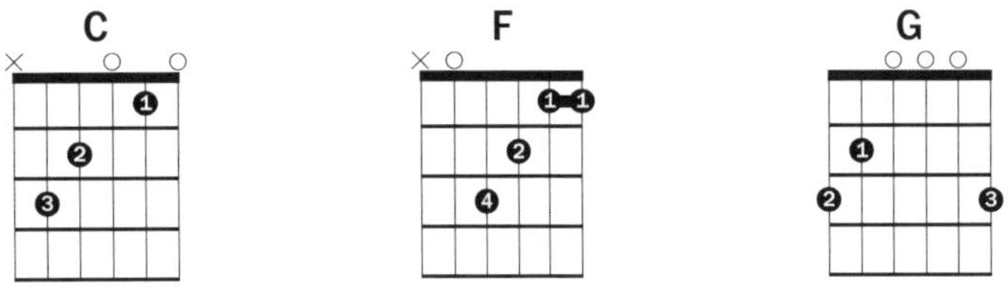

arr. John Hartin

I went across the river, and I lay down to sleep
I went across the river, and I lay down to sleep
When I woke up, had shackles on my feet.

Twenty nine links of chain around my leg
Twenty nine links of chain around my leg
And on each link, the initial of my name.

I asked that judge, tell me, what might be my fine
I asked that judge, tell me, what might be my fine
Twenty one years on the R C Mountain line.

The train arrived, sixteen coaches long
The train arrived, sixteen coaches long
The girl I love is on that train and gone.

If anyone asks you who composed this song
If anyone asks you who composed this song
Tell 'em t'was I, and I sing it all day long.

Careless Love

I first heard this song sung by June Carter Cash. I consider it a country music staple. The accompaniment is in Johnny Cash-style with a boom-chicka-boom rhythm.

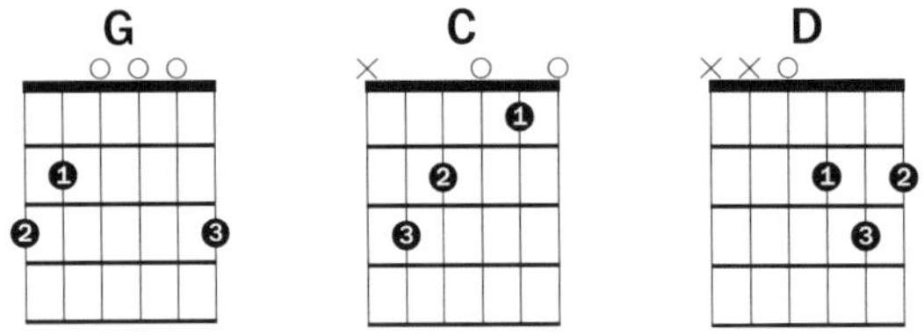

11
C
C
G
care - less love. See what
14
D
G
love has done to me.

The Crawdad Song

I first heard this classic tune on a recording by the rock and country legend, Jerry Lee Lewis. Remember, the p stands for pull-off. Raise your finger off the string to "pull off" it. The accompaniment is in a Johnny Cash-style with a boom-chicka-boom rhythm.

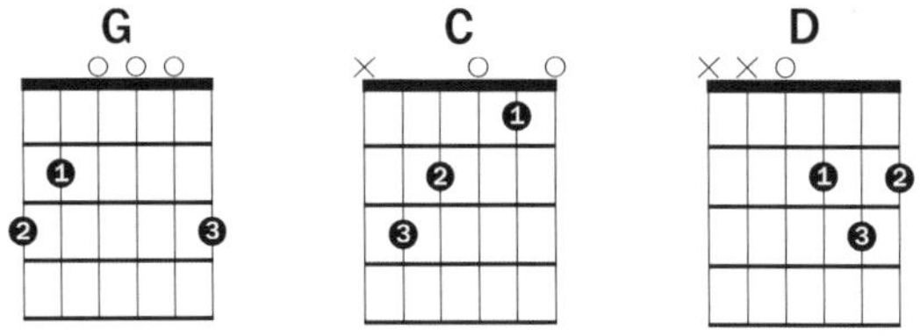

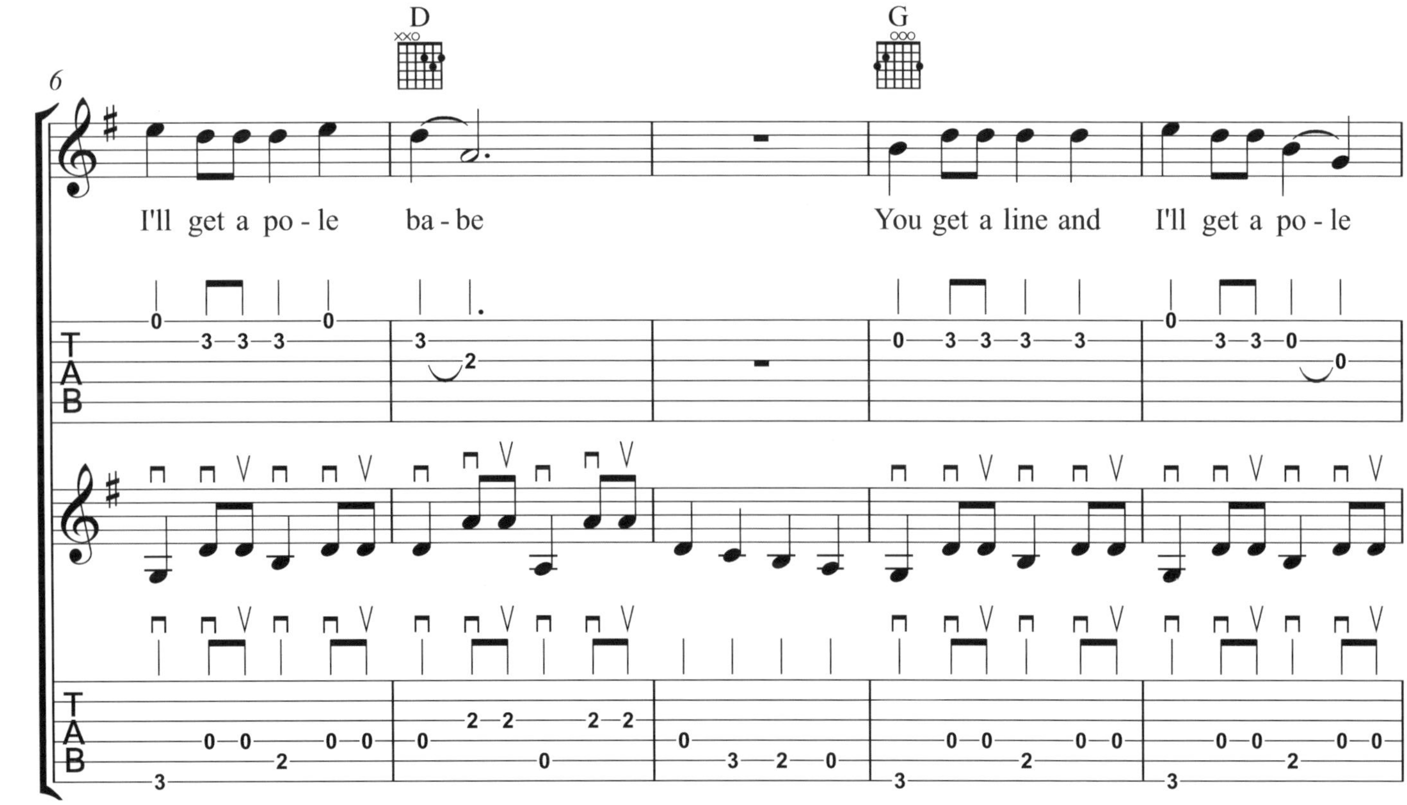

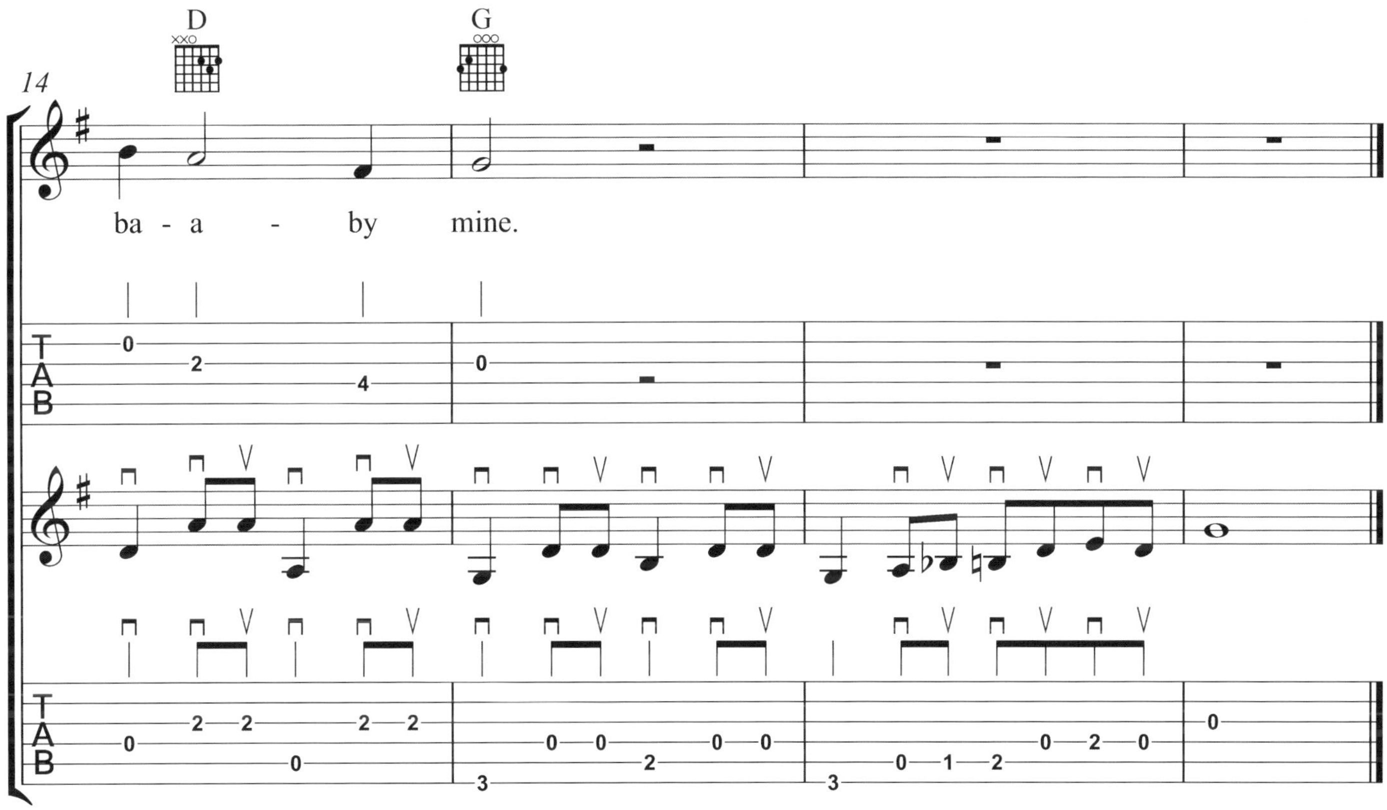

The last two measures of the accompaniment are a go-to country lick!

The Unclouded Day

This great gospel tune has been performed by Johnny Cash, Willie Nelson, Toby Keith and many other artists.

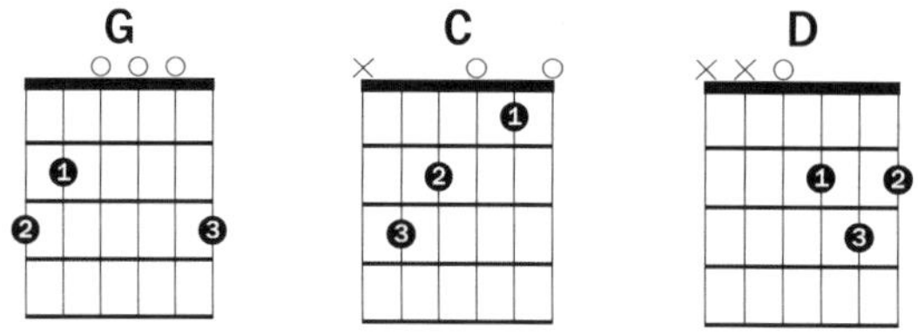

If you need some ideas for accompaniment, check out these great play-along patterns:

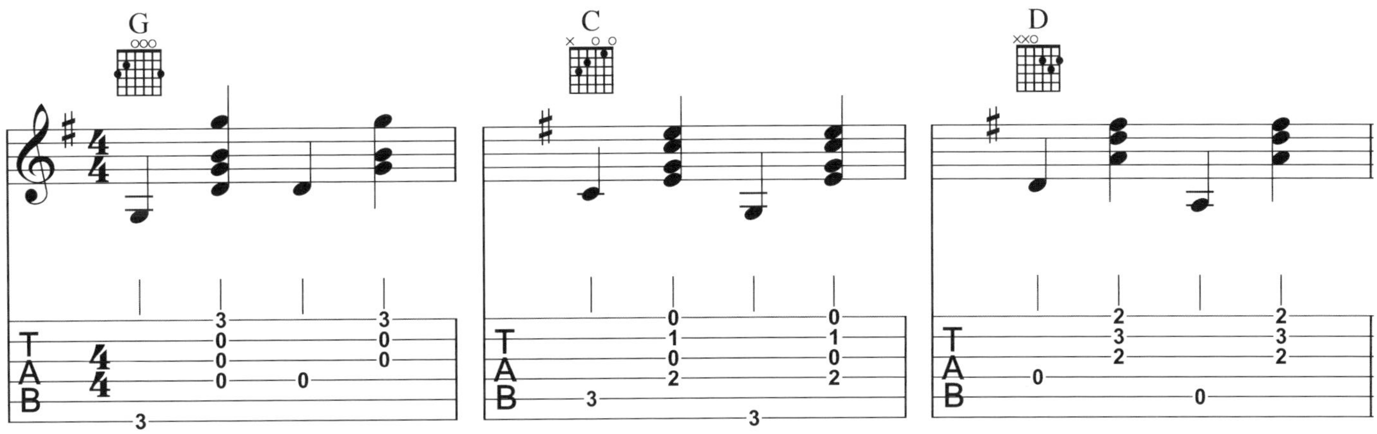

Amazing Grace

Amazing Grace has such a beautiful melody. You can play the chords in a waltz time with a single bass note followed by two strums.

11

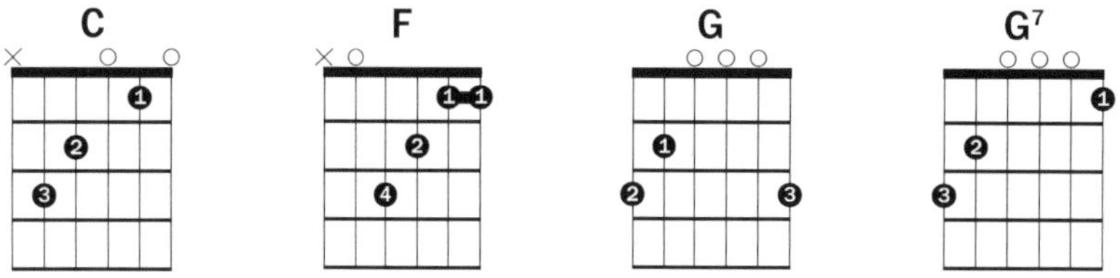

arr. John Hartin

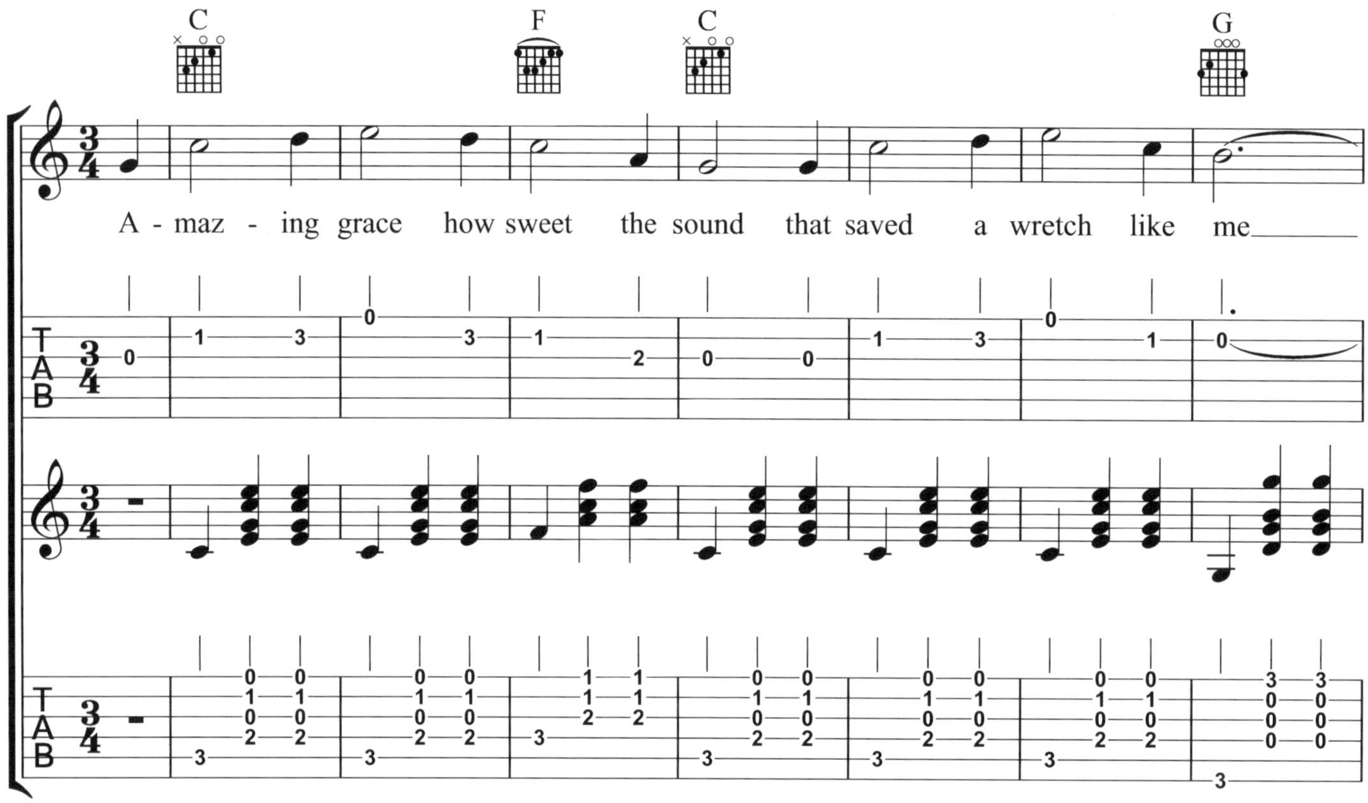

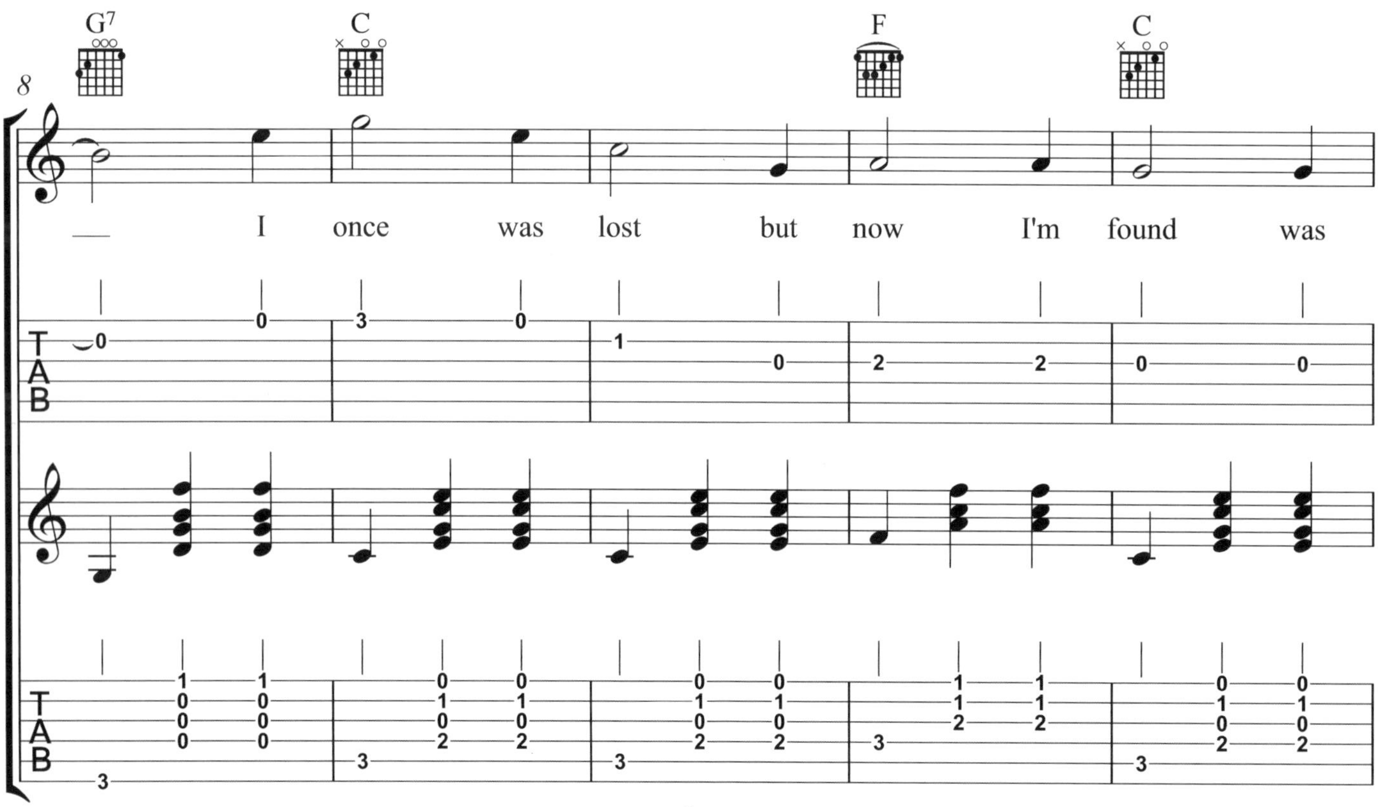

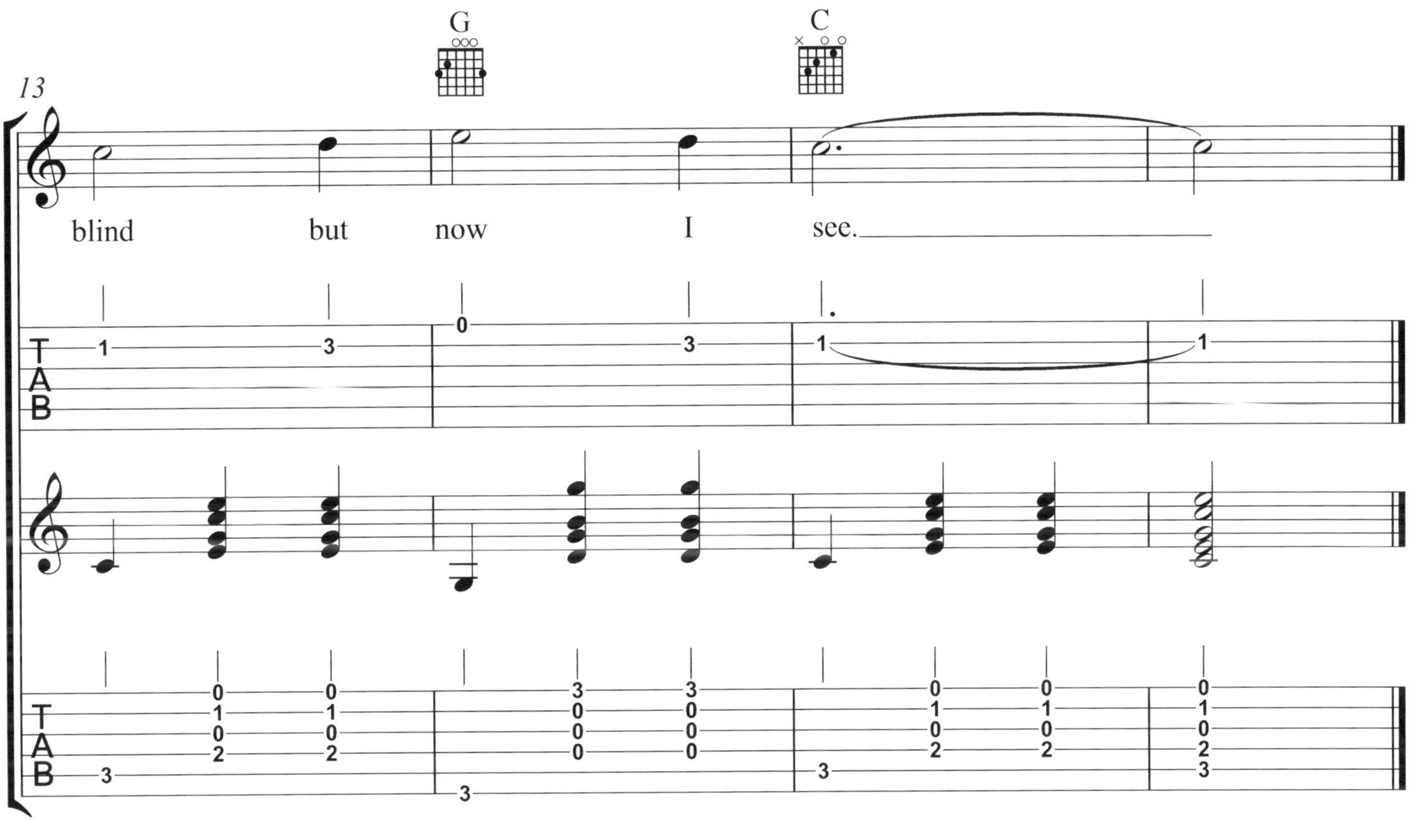

You can also play this tune by combining single melody notes with chords in the chord-melody style:

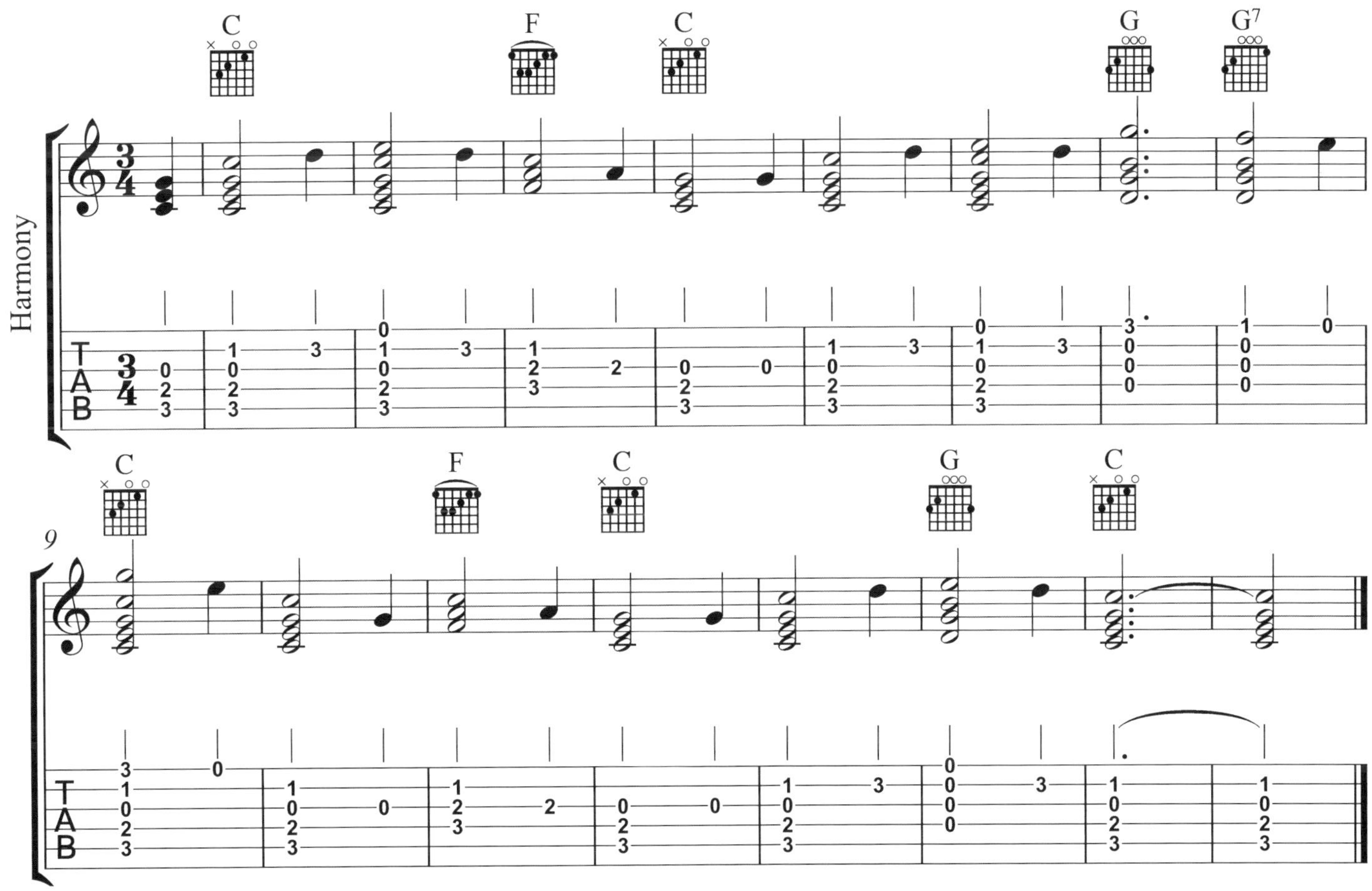

In the Pines

"Coal Miner's Daughter" was about the life and career of country singer, Loretta Lynn. You may remember Sissy Spacek singing this timeless country favorite in the film.

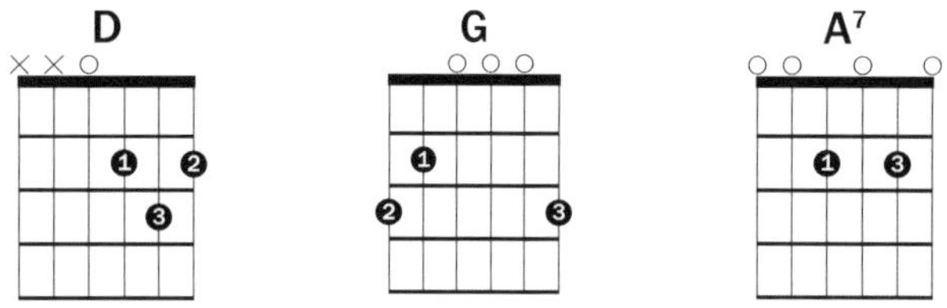

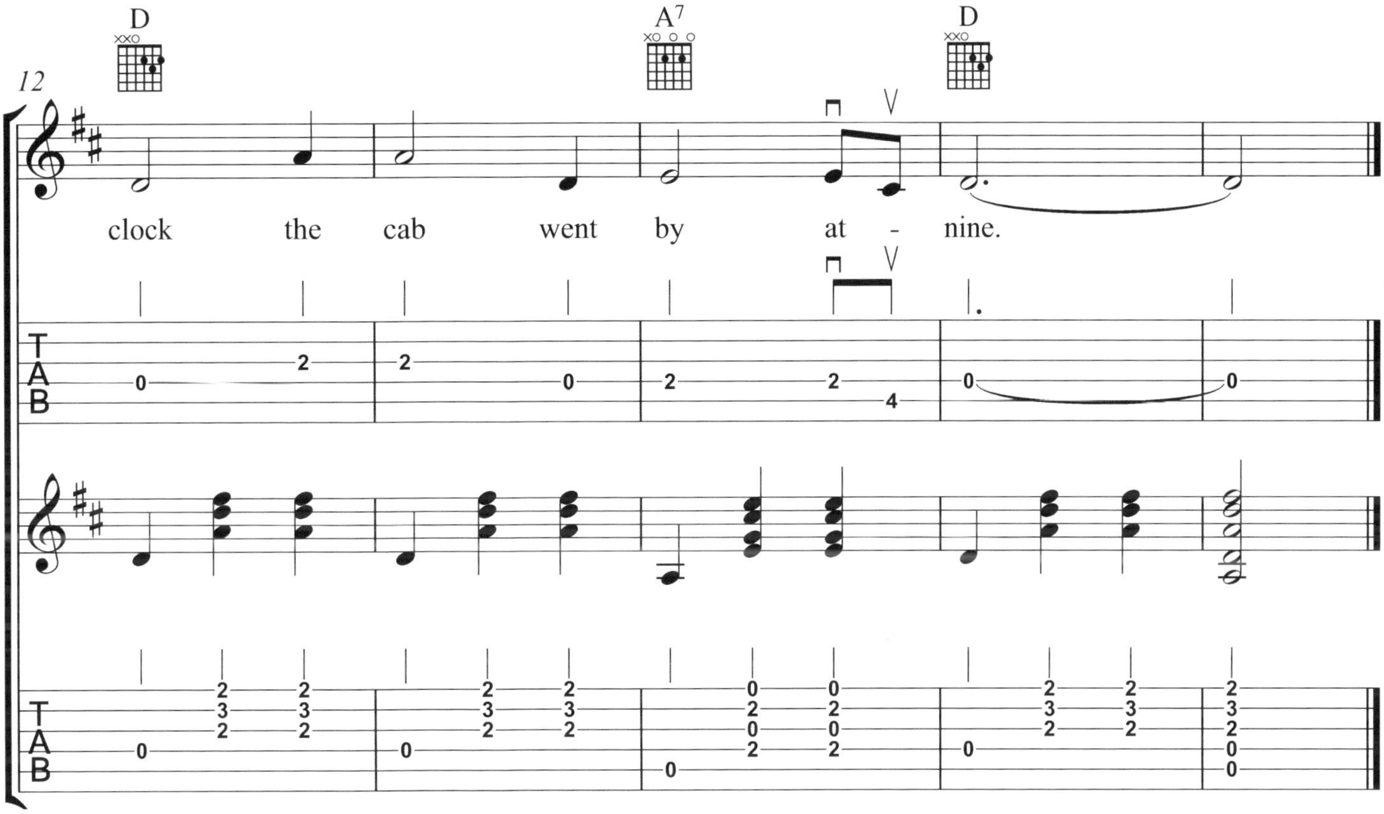

I asked my captain for the time of day
He said he throwed his watch away
A long steel rail and a short cross tie
I'm on my way back home

Little girl, little girl, what have I done
That makes you treat me so
You caused me to weep, you caused me to mourn
You caused me to leave my home

My father was an engineer
Died a mile out of town
His head was found in the driving gear
But his body was never found

Oklahoma Moonlight Waltz

I wrote this song after playing a show in McAlester, Oklahoma with Rusty Hudelson and The Knights of the West. The moon was mighty pretty, so it needed a special song.

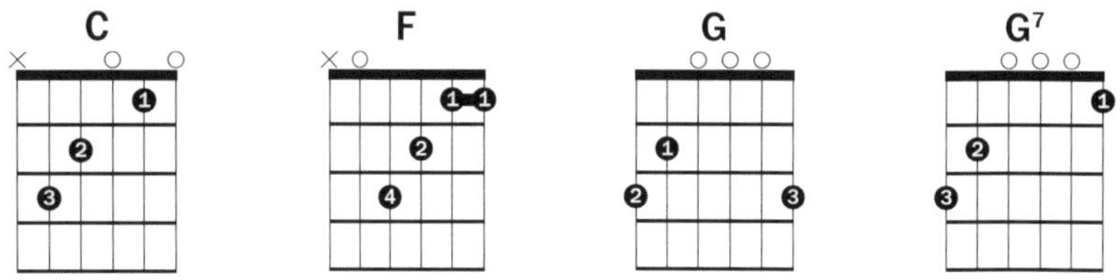

John Hartin

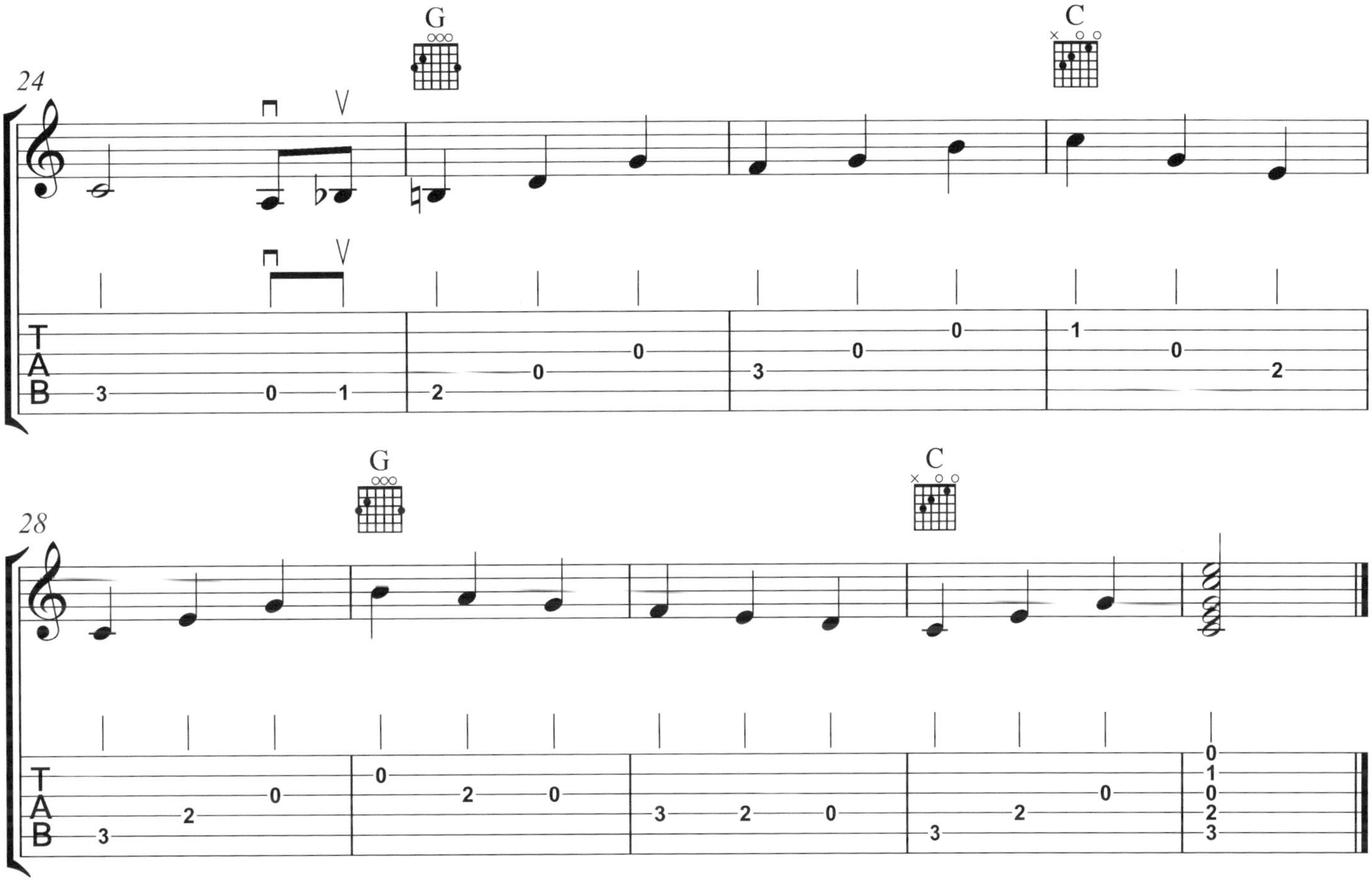
24
G
C
TAB
28
G
C
TAB

Hand Me Down My Walking Cane

I first heard this tune on a recording by Jerry Lee Lewis and then later by Porter Wagoner. It's a classic country tune and fun to play! The accompaniment is in "shuffle style".

14

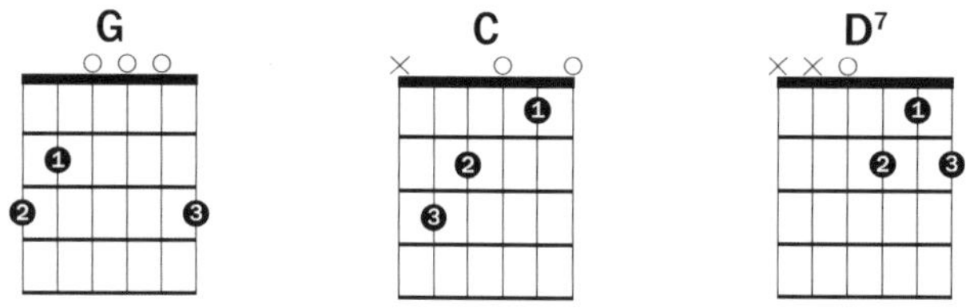

James A. Bland

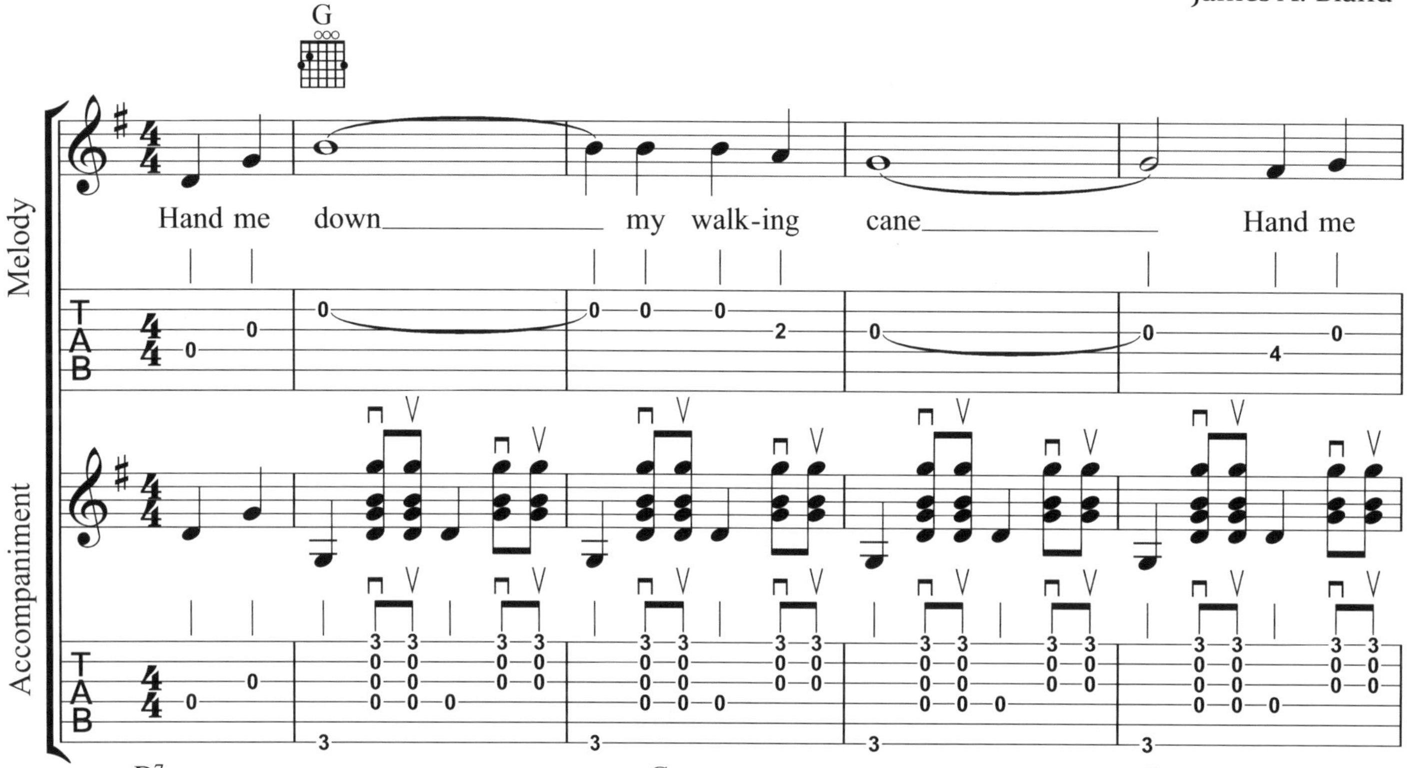

10
G
cane I'm gon - na catch that mid - night train all my
13
D7
G
sins are tak - en a - way.

Scoot-a-Boot Boogie

I wrote this tune for a student of mine. Try playing it with a shuffle rhythm of all up/down strokes to really get the dance floor shaking.

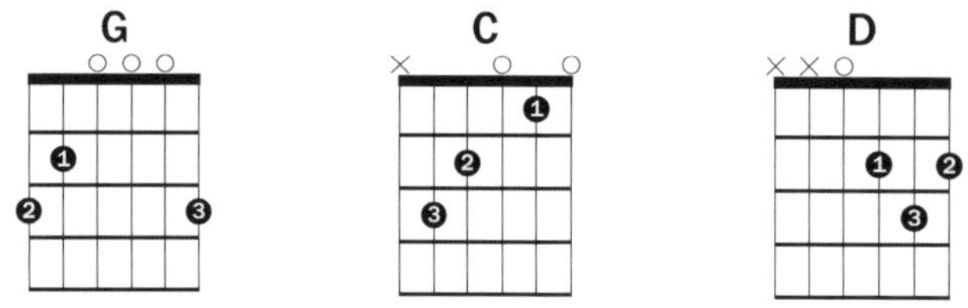

John Hartin

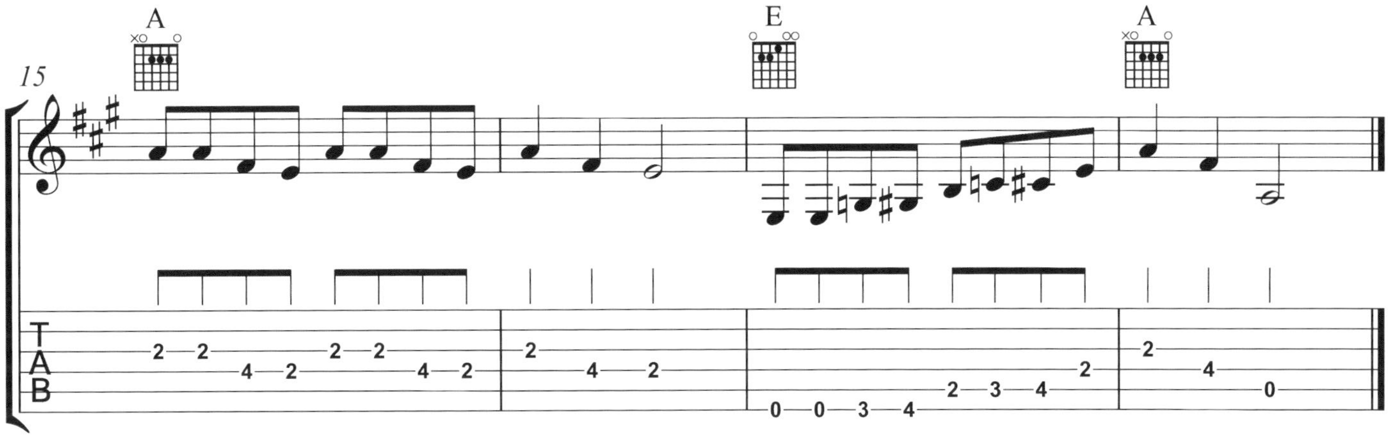

Try it with this shuffle rhythm accompaniment.

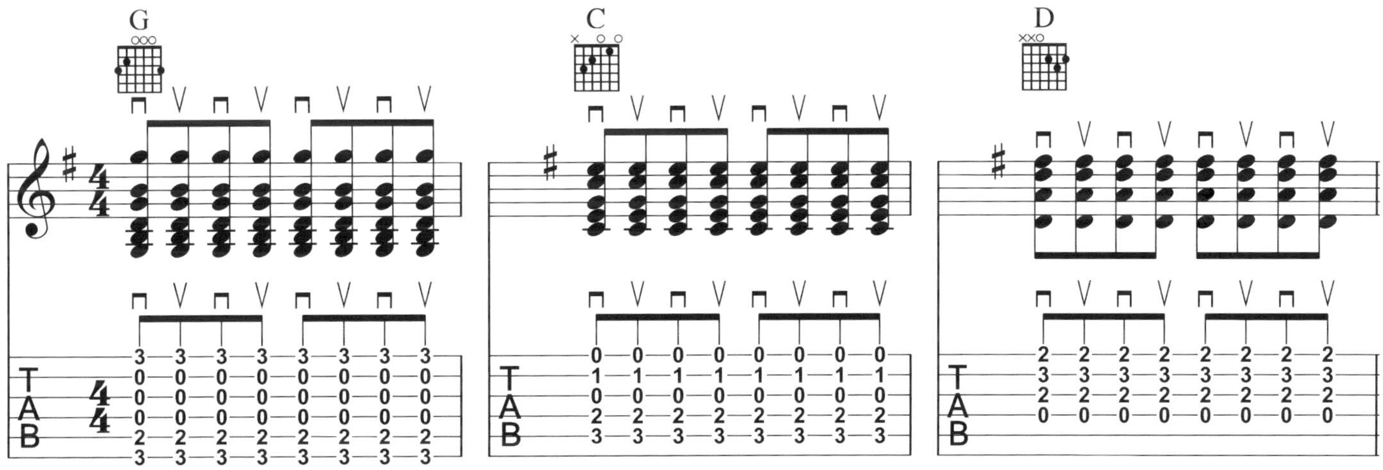

Lone Star Country

I wrote this as a fun dance tune. Texas is the Lone-Star State, so I tried to put a little Texas dance-hall flavor in this tune. It has a few challenging licks, so take your Texas time playing it.

16

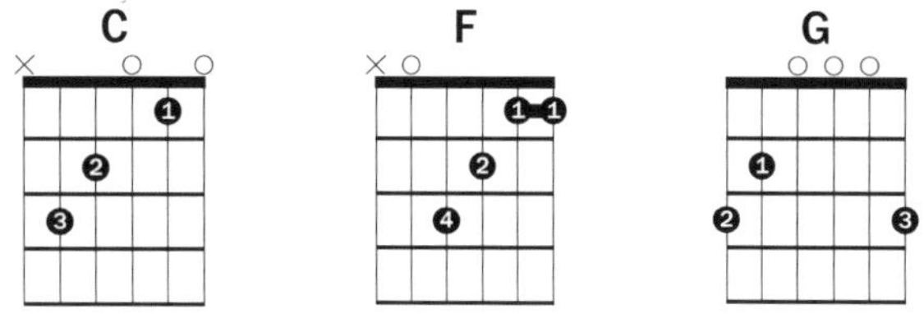

John Hartin

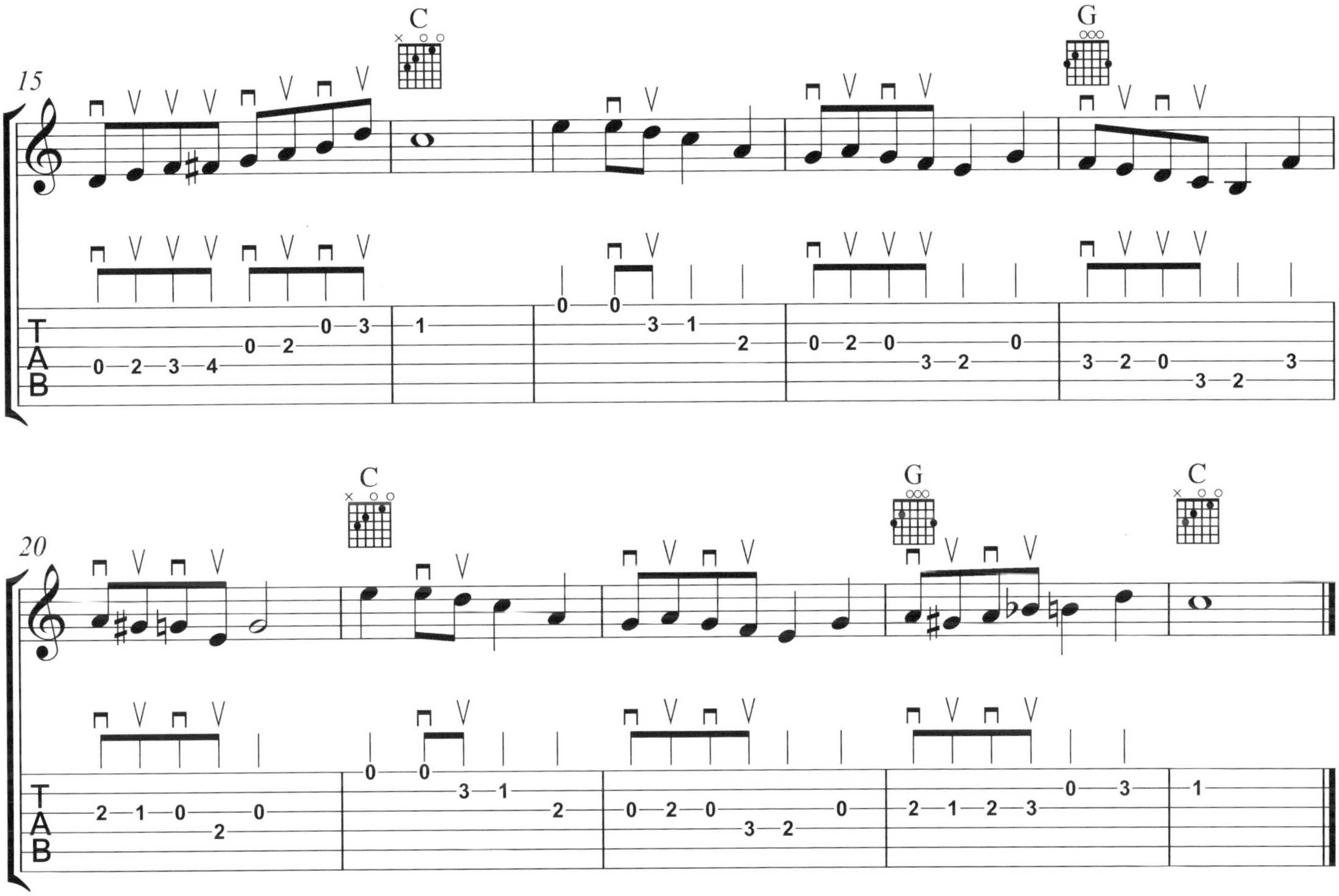
15
C
G
TAB
20
C
G
C
TAB

Foggy Mountain Top

Lester Flatt, Earl Scruggs, and Maybell Carter all had great arrangements of this tune. Although Earl was a world-famous banjo picker, he was also an accomplished guitarist.

17

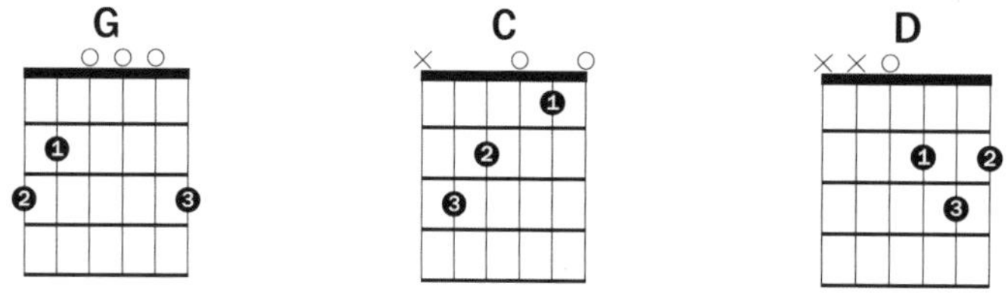

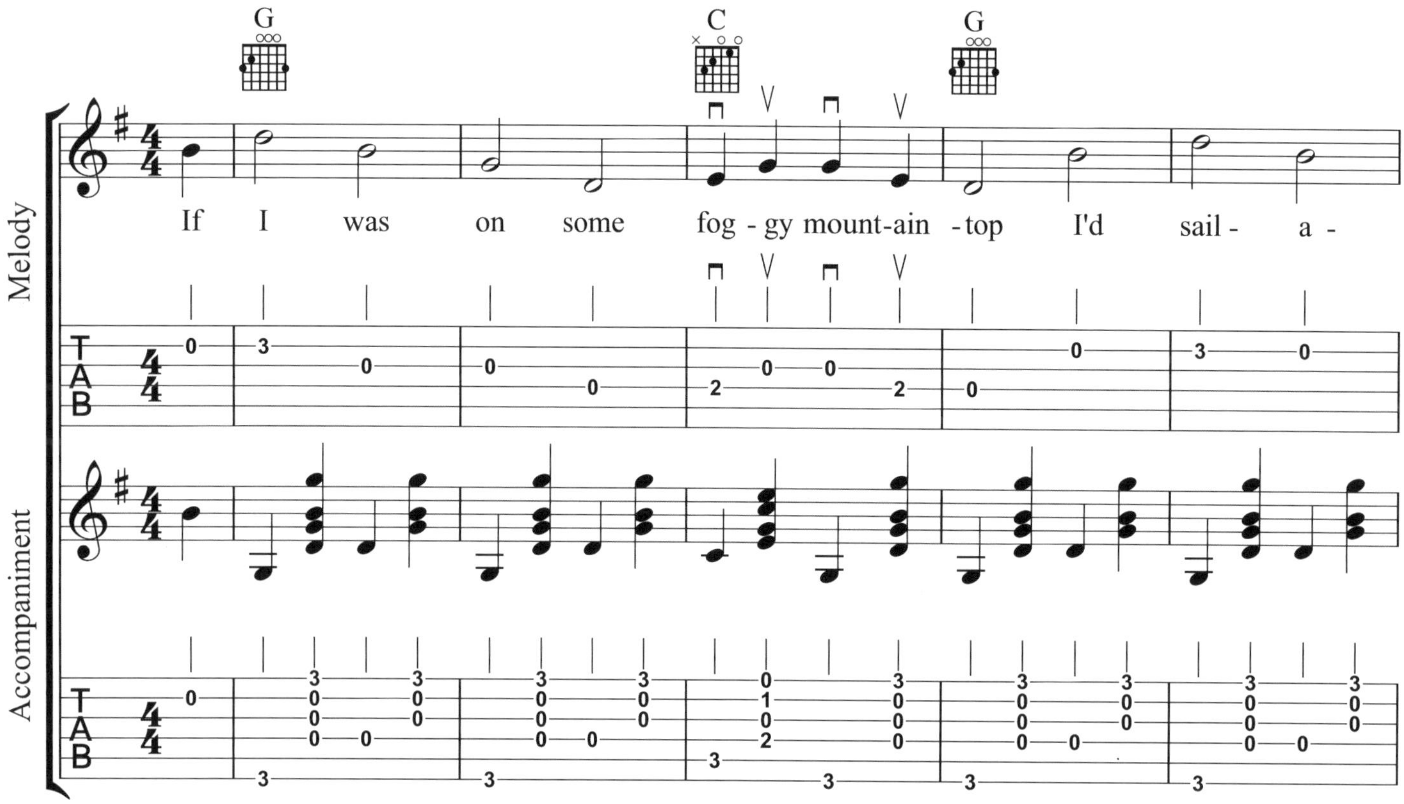

If I had listened what mama says
I would not have been here today
A-lying around this old jail house
A-weeping my sweet life away

Oh, if you see that girl of mine
There's something you must tell her
She need not be foolin' no time away
To court some other feller

Oh, she caused me to weep and she caused me to mourn
She caused me to leave my home
Oh, the lonesome pines and the good old times
I'm on my way back home

Now if you see that girl of mine
There's something you can tell her
She need not fool her time away
To court some other feller

Old-Time Religion

Johnny Cash, Willie Nelson, The Statler Brothers and The Mormon Tabernacle Choir have recorded this classic country tune.

18

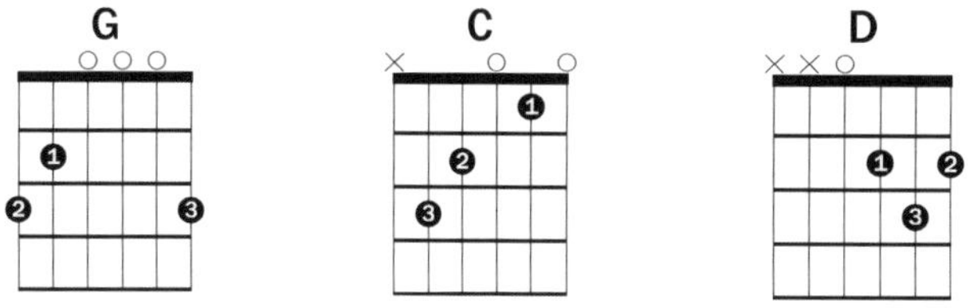

Under the Double Eagle

This has been a great guitar song for many years. I get requests for this song frequently and my students really enjoy playing it. Try to hold the chords during each measure.

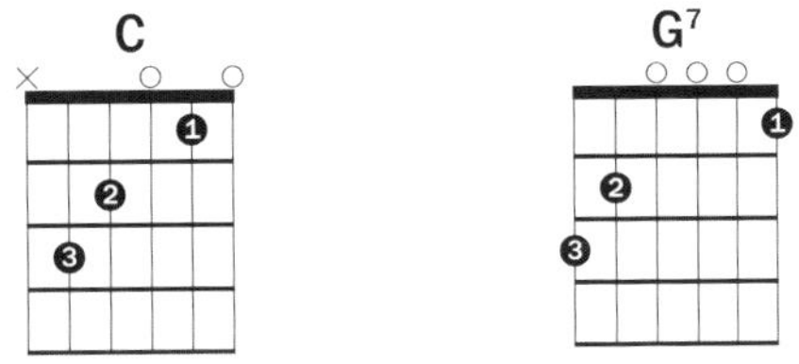

arr. John Hartin

Wildwood Flower

This is an important song in the history of country music. It was written by A. P. Carter of the famous Carter Family.

20

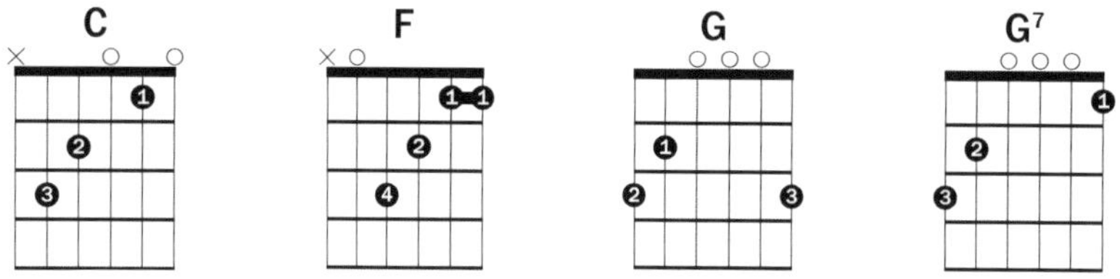

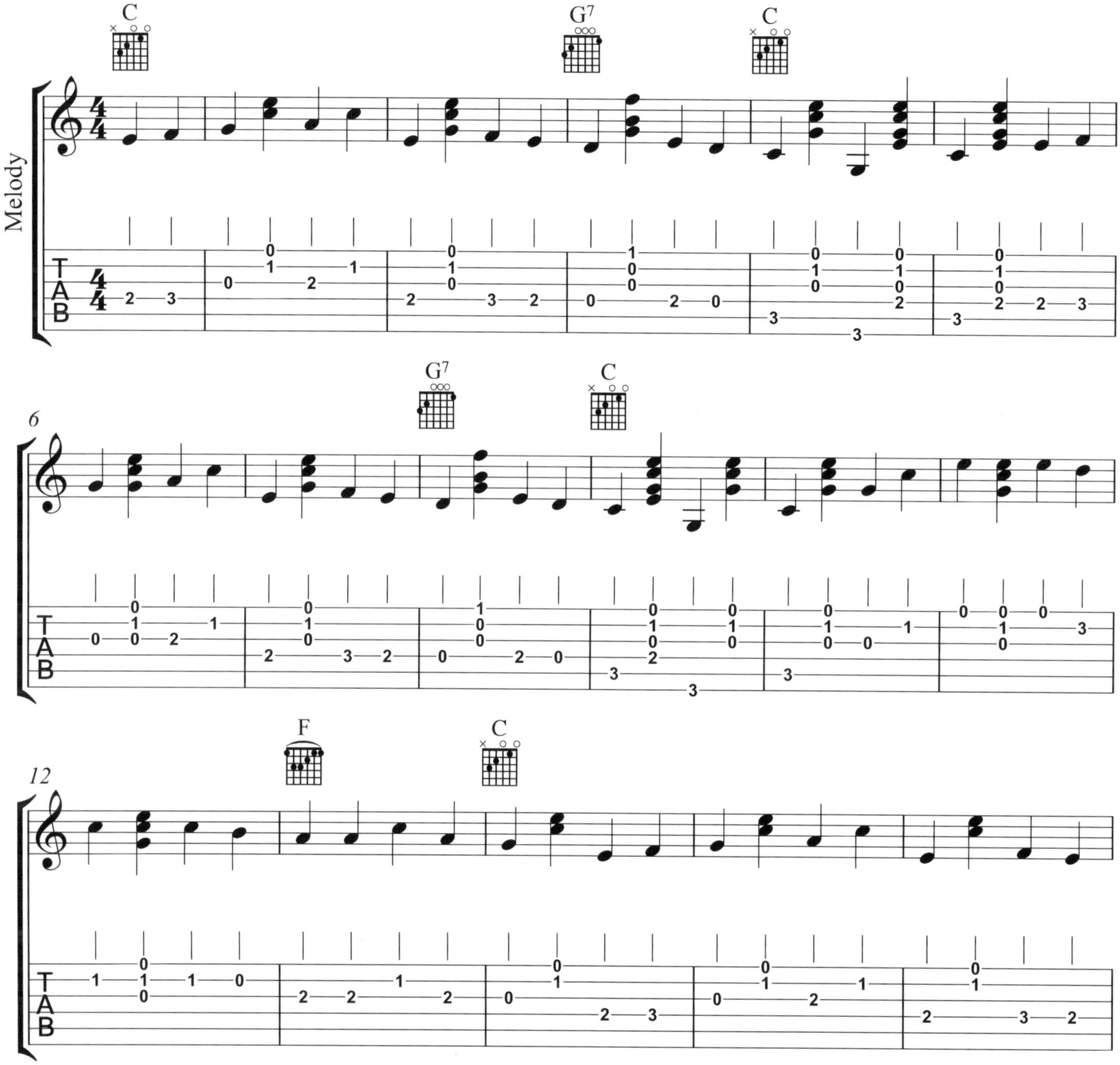

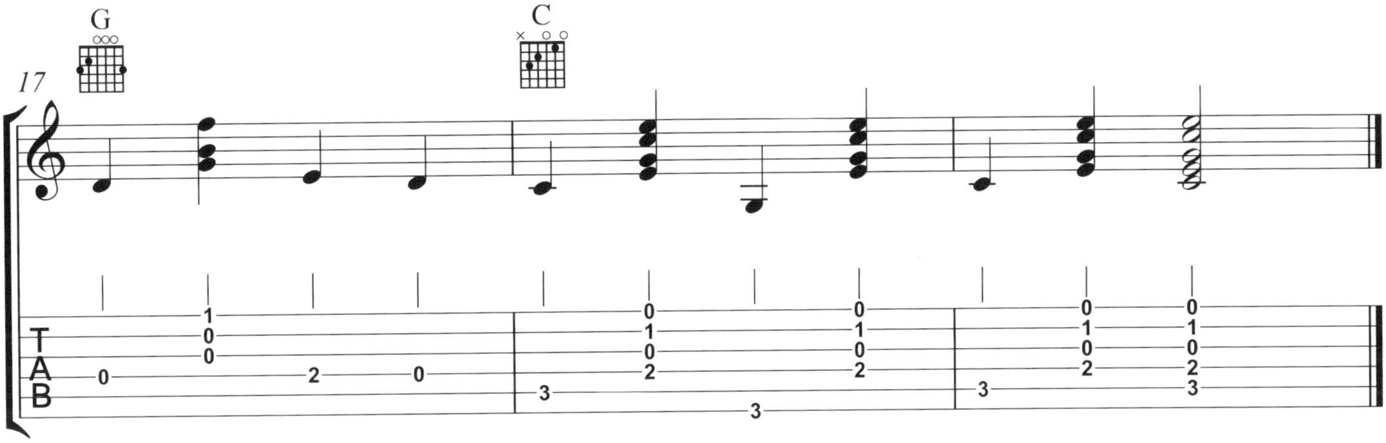

I will twine, I will mingle my raven black hair
With the roses so red and the lilies so fair
And the myrtle so bright with it's emerald hue
The pale and the leader and eyes look like blue

I will dance, I will sing and my laugh shall be gay
I will charm every heart, in his crown I will sway
When I awoke from my dreaming my idol was clay
All portion of love had all flown away

Oh, he taught me to love him and promised to love
And to cherish me over all others above
How my heart is now wondering no misery can tell
He's left with no warning, no word of farewell

Oh, he taught me to love him and called me his flower
That was blooming to cheer him through life's dreary hour
Oh, I long to see him and regret the dark hour
He's one that neglected this pale wildwood flower

About The Authors

John Hartin

John Hartin is widely known as the architect of the Country and Bluegrass music degree program at South Plains College in Levelland, Texas. Under John's leadership, the program became known worldwide, and has many famous graduates. John holds a Bachelor's degree from Briar Cliff University and a Master's from Wayland Baptist University. He has been inducted into the Buddy Holly Terrace Hall of Fame, the West Texas Hall of Fame, and both the Nebraska and Iowa Rock and Roll Halls of Fame. He has been a member of the Mel Bay Advisory Board, as well as the Commercial Music Advisory Board at South Plains College. John retired after 28 successful years at South Plains College and is now a partner at Texas Music Supply where he still teaches students every week on guitar, pedal steel, banjo, Dobro®, and mandolin.

Chet Hartin

Chester "Chet" Travis Hartin - was named after two great country guitarists (Chet Atkins and Merle Travis). Chet started playing gigs when he was fourteen and hasn't stopped. An accomplished bass and keyboard player, he's always learning a new instrument (steel guitar, accordion, banjo, mandolin, bagpipes, etc). He appears on several albums and has been very active in the New York and Chicago music scenes. When not playing music, you can usually find him on a computer doing his second most favorite thing - programming, in that capacity he's worked for several large firms, including CBS and Amazon Web Services.